GoodFood

101 BUDGET DISHES

Published in 2009 by BBC Books,
an imprint of Ebury Publishing
A Random House Group company

Recipes © BBC Magazines 2009
Photographs © BBC Magazines 2009
Book design © Woodlands Books Ltd 2009
All recipes contained within this book first
appeared in BBC *Good Food* magazine.

The Random House Group Limited
Reg. No. 954009

Addresses for companies within the
Random House Group can be found at
www.randomhouse.co.uk

A CIP catalogue record for this book is available
from the British Library.

The Random House Group Limited supports
The Forest Stewardship Council (FSC), the
leading international forest certification organization.
All our titles that are printed on Greenpeace
approved FSC certified paper carry the FSC logo.
Our paper procurement policy can be found at
www.rbooks.co.uk/environment

To buy books by your favourite authors and
register for offers visit www.rbooks.co.uk

Printed and bound by Firmengruppe APPL,
aprinta druck, Wemding, Germany
Colour origination by Dot Gradations Ltd, UK

Commissioning Editor: Lorna Russell
Project Editor: Laura Higginson
Designer: Annette Peppis
Jacket Design: Kathryn Gammon
Production: Phil Spencer
Picture Researcher: Gabby Harrington

ISBN: 9781846077227

10 9 8 7 6 5 4 3

GoodFood

101 BUDGET DISHES
TRIPLE-TESTED RECIPES

Editor
Jane Hornby

Contents

Introduction

We're all more aware of food costs these days, but good cooking on a budget is familiar territory at *Good Food* magazine. For years we've been inspiring cooks pressed for time and money and this collection is packed with some of our favourite ways to cut costs, not taste.

This handy book holds the key to quick, good-value recipes and filling family classics, plus brilliant ideas for packed lunches and leftovers. As well as making your money stretch further, with our make-you-own suggestions and helpful nutritional analysis, you'll know exactly what you're eating.

Thrifty cooking goes hand in hand with shopping seasonally, so get to know what's best when. Canny cooks also make the most of storecupboard and frozen ingredients. We'll also show you how to make cheaper cuts of good quality free-range meat go further.

On a final note, a third of all food bought ends up in the bin. That's a third of your hard-earned budget! So make a shopping list with *101 Budget Dishes* in hand and you'll be saving money – and reducing waste – before you know it.

Jane

Jane Hornby
Good Food magazine

Notes and conversion tables

NOTES ON THE RECIPES
• Eggs are large in the UK and Australia and extra large in America unless stated otherwise.
• Wash fresh produce before preparation.
• Recipes contain nutritional analyses for 'sugar', which means the total sugar content including all natural sugars in the ingredients unless otherwise stated.

OVEN TEMPERATURES

Gas	°C	Fan °C	°F	Oven temp.
¼	110	90	225	Very cool
½	120	100	250	Very cool
1	140	120	275	Cool or slow
2	150	130	300	Cool or slow
3	160	140	325	Warm
4	180	160	350	Moderate
5	190	170	375	Moderately hot
6	200	180	400	Fairly hot
7	220	200	425	Hot
8	230	210	450	Very hot
9	240	220	475	Very hot

APPROXIMATE WEIGHT CONVERSIONS
• All the recipes in this book list both imperial and metric measurements. Conversions are approximate and have been rounded up or down. Follow one set of measurements only; do not mix the two.
• Cup measurements, which are used by cooks in Australia and America, have not been listed here as they vary from ingredient to ingredient. Kitchen scales should be used to measure dry/solid ingredients.

Good Food are concerned about sustainable sourcing and animal welfare so where possible, we use organic ingredients, humanely-reared meats, free-range chickens and eggs and unrefined sugar.

SPOON MEASURES

Spoon measurements are level unless otherwise specified.

- 1 teaspoon (tsp) = 5ml
- 1 tablespoon (tbsp) = 15ml
- 1 Australian tablespoon = 20ml (cooks in Australia should measure 3 teaspoons where 1 tablespoon is specified in a recipe)

APPROXIMATE LIQUID CONVERSIONS

metric	Imperial	AUS	US
50ml	2fl oz	¼ cup	¼ cup
125ml	4fl oz	½ cup	½ cup
175ml	6fl oz	¾ cup	¾ cup
225ml	8fl oz	1 cup	1 cup
300ml	10fl oz/½ pint	½ pint	1¼ cups
450ml	16fl oz	2 cups	2 cups/1 pint
600ml	20fl oz/1 pint	1 pint	2½ cups
1 litre	35fl oz/1¾ pints	1¾ pints	1 quart

A tasty topping of melting cheese and tangy onions transforms chops into something far more exciting.

Cheese and onion pork chops

4 pork chops
2 tsp olive oil
1 tsp English mustard
4 tbsp caramelized onions, from a jar
50g/2oz Cheshire cheese, grated
1 tsp thyme, chopped

Take 20 minutes • Serves 4

1 Heat grill to High, then place the chops on a grill pan, rub with oil and season. Grill for about 6 minutes on each side, until golden.
2 Spread a little mustard over one side of each chop, then top each one with 1 tablespoon of onions. Mix together the cheese and thyme, sprinkle over the chops, then grill until golden and bubbly.

• Per serving 378 kcalories, protein 36g, carbohydrate 8g, fat 23g, saturated fat 9g, fibre none, sugar 6g, salt 0.56g

Apples, sausages and bacon are a marriage made in heaven – just think about roast pork with apple sauce!

Sticky apple, sausages and bacon

8 rashers smoked streaky bacon
8 quality pork sausages
1 tbsp sunflower oil
2 red-skinned apples, each cut into 8 wedges
mashed potatoes, to serve

Takes 35 minutes • Serves 4

1 Preheat oven to 220°C/fan 200°C/gas 7. Wrap a piece of bacon around each sausage. Heat the oil in a flameproof roasting tin on the hob, then brown the bacon-wrapped sausages in the tin. Place in the oven and roast for 20 minutes.

2 Toss in the apple wedges and roast everything for another 10 minutes until the sausages are cooked and the apples are sticky and caramelized. Serve with mashed potatoes.

• Per serving 442 kcalories, protein 22g, carbohydrate 14g, fat 34g, saturated fat 11g, fibre 1g, sugar 10g, salt 2.72g

There's so much flavour packed into this beany bake that your meat-eating guests will be just as happy as the veggies.

Butter bean and squash crumble

350g/12oz dried butter beans, soaked overnight in cold water
4 tbsp olive oil
2 onions, chopped
4 garlic cloves, finely chopped
1–2 red chillies, seeded and finely chopped
700g jar passata
1 dried bouquet garni
425ml/¾ pint white wine
425ml/¾ pint vegetable stock
700g/1lb 9oz squash, peeled, seeded and cut into chunks

FOR THE CRUMBLE
50g/2oz breadcrumbs
25g/1oz walnuts, finely chopped
1 tbsp chopped rosemary
4 tbsp chopped parsley

Takes 2¼ hours • Serves 6

1 Rinse the beans and put in a large pan with plenty of water to cover. Bring to the boil, reduce the heat and cook, partly covered, for about 1 hour until tender. Drain well.
2 Heat 2 tablespoons of the oil in a large pan, add the onions, fry for 10 minutes until lightly browned. Add the garlic, chillies, passata, bouquet garni, wine, stock, salt and pepper, and bring to the boil. Reduce the heat and simmer, uncovered, for 20 minutes, then add the squash and cook for a further 20 minutes. Taste and add more seasoning, if necessary.
3 Preheat oven to 180°C/fan 160°C/gas 4. Stir the beans into the sauce, then transfer to a 2.5-litre gratin dish, or two smaller ones. Mix together all the crumble ingredients, plus the remaining 2 tablespoons of oil, then sprinkle over the beans. Bake for 30 minutes until the topping is golden and crisp.

• Per serving 428 kcalories, protein 17g, carbohydrate 62g, fat 12g, saturated fat 2g, fibre 13g, sugar 18g, salt 0.93g

Whole chicken legs are substantially cheaper than breast meat – and are full of flavour, too. Serve this filling supper with warm flatbreads or plain rice.

Chicken with roots and chickpeas

4 chicken legs
2 tbsp olive oil
4 carrots, cut into large chunks
3 parsnips, cut into large chunks
1 onion, cut into large chunks
1 tbsp Moroccan seasoning or mix
1tsp each of ground cumin,
coriander and cinnamon
440g can chickpeas, rinsed and
drained
400g can tomatoes
chopped coriander leaves (optional)

Takes 1 hour • Serves 4

1 Preheat oven to 220°C/fan 200°C/gas 7. Toss the chicken, oil, vegetables and seasoning together with some salt and pepper. Roast for 40 minutes, shaking the pan every so often.
2 When the chicken and vegetables are cooked, lift the chicken on to four plates and keep warm, then put the roasting tin over a high heat on the hob. Tip in the chickpeas and tomatoes and bring to a simmer. Cook for a few minutes, then stir in the coriander, if using. Serve with the chicken.

• Per serving 590 kcalories, protein 40g, carbohydrate 37g, fat 32g, saturated fat 8g, fibre 10g, sugar 17g, salt 2.12g

A spicy, slowly simmered chilli is hard to beat on top of a fluffy jacket potato or pile of rice. You could even use it for a spicy cottage pie.

Chilli con carne

2 tbsp olive oil
1 onion, finely chopped
1 carrot, finely chopped
1 celery stick, finely chopped
500g pack lean minced beef
½–1 tsp chilli powder or chilli flakes
2 garlic cloves, crushed
2 tsp dried mixed herbs
small glass of milk
2 × 400g cans chopped tomatoes
large glass of white wine or stock
2 tbsp tomato purée
2–3 roasted red peppers from a jar or deli counter, chopped (optional)
400g can red kidney beans, drained and rinsed

Takes 1½ hours • Serves 4

1 Heat the oil in a large pan with a well-fitting lid. Add the onion, carrot and celery, cover and fry for 5 minutes until the vegetables are softened and lightly coloured. Remove the lid and tip in the beef, breaking it up with a wooden spoon, then fry over a fairly high heat, stirring all the time until it is evenly coloured. Add the chilli, garlic and herbs and fry for 1 minute more.

2 Reduce the heat, pour in the milk, stir well, then simmer for a few minutes, stirring occasionally, until the milk has almost evaporated. Stir in the tomatoes, wine (or stock) and tomato purée with some seasoning, then bring to the boil. Reduce the heat then simmer for 1 hour. Stir in the peppers (if using) and kidney beans, simmer for 5 minutes more, then serve.

• Per serving 447 kcalories, protein 37g, carbohydrate 27g, fat 20g, saturated fat 7g, fibre 8g, sugar 14g, salt 2.17g

This tasty chicken one-pot with chorizo can be prepared ahead and just reheated and plonked on the table. Serve this with garlic bread and a big salad, or a few slices of avocado and a squeeze of lime.

Chilli chicken one-pot

2 large onions, halved and sliced
2 tbsp olive oil
265g chorizo ring, skinned and thickly sliced
4 red peppers, seeded and cut into large chunks
2 × 400g cans chopped tomatoes
2 chicken stock cubes
½–1 tsp dried chilli flakes
2 tsp dried oregano
16 large boneless skinless chicken thighs
3 × 410g cans red kidney beans, drained
small pack coriander, chopped, to serve

Takes 1½ hours • Serves 8

1 Preheat oven to 180°C/fan 160°C/gas 4. Fry the onions in the oil for 5 minutes. Add the chorizo and fry for 2 minutes more. Stir in the peppers, tomatoes, a can of water, the stock cubes, chilli and oregano.
2 Sit the chicken thighs in the sauce, bring to a simmer then remove from the heat. Cover and bake in the oven for 40 minutes. Add the beans, stir, then return to the oven for 20 minutes more. Stir in the coriander to serve.

• Per serving 501 kcalories, protein 58g, carbohydrate 30g, fat 18g, saturated fat 6g, fibre 9g, sugar 14g, salt 3.16g

Quorn is a great please-all choice if you have vegetarians and meat-eaters in the same household.

Quorn and carrot pilaf

3 tbsp vegetable oil
1 large onion, chopped
1 large aubergine, cubed
1 garlic clove, crushed
3 tbsp balti curry paste
1 large sweet potato, cubed
250g/9oz carrots, grated
250g/9oz frozen beans
350g/12oz basmati rice
300ml/½ pint reduced-fat coconut milk
200g bag spinach leaves
2 × 140g packs low-fat Quorn fajita strips

Takes 45 minutes • Serves 4 generously

1 Heat the oil in a large pan. Add the onion and cook for 5 minutes until softened but not browned. Stir in the aubergine and cook for 5 minutes, adding the garlic and curry paste 1 minute before the end of the cooking time.
2 Stir in the sweet potato, carrots, beans, rice, 700ml of water and the coconut milk. Bring to the boil, cover and simmer for 15 minutes.
3 Add the spinach and Quorn strips to the pan, stir everything together, then cover and leave off the heat for 5 minutes. Fork through to fluff up the rice, then serve.

• Per serving 699 kcalories, protein 22.7g, carbohydrate 106.2g, fat 23.6g, saturated fat 8.8g, fibre 12.6g, sugar 18.5g, salt 2.26g

This delicious pasta sauce is packed with healthy veg – but they'll never guess! It's good food and good value too.

Good-for-you bolognese

2 tsp olive oil
1 onion, chopped
4 carrots, chopped
2 courgettes, chopped
85g/3oz mushrooms
1 garlic clove, crushed
400g can chopped tomatoes
1 tbsp Worcestershire sauce
500g/1lb 2oz lean minced beef
a handful of basil leaves
1 tbsp gravy granules
400g/14oz spaghetti

Takes 45 minutes • Serves 4–6

1 Heat the oil in a large frying pan and add the onion. Cook gently for a few minutes, then add the carrots, courgettes and mushrooms, and fry for 5 more minutes. Stir in the garlic 1 minute before the end of the cooking time.
2 Tip in the tomatoes, Worcestershire sauce and 300ml of boiling water, then season. Bring to the boil, cover, then simmer for 15 minutes. Meanwhile, fry the mince in a non-stick pan for 10 minutes, stirring until browned all over.
3 Add most of the basil leaves to the veg sauce, then blend until smooth. Pour the sauce and gravy granules into the mince, then stir to thicken. Cover and simmer for 15 minutes.
4 Meanwhile, cook the pasta in a pan of lightly salted boiling water according to the packet instructions. When just tender, reserve a small cup of the cooking water, then drain. Mix the spaghetti sauce and reserved water, and serve topped with the remaining basil leaves.

• Per serving (4) 597 kcalories, protein 43g, carbohydrate 89g, fat 10g, saturated fat 3g, fibre 7g, sugar 16g, salt 0.9g

You can sneak a few vegetables that might normally be refused into this scrumptious supper, which won't break the bank.

Pesto chicken kebabs with roasted veg pasta

about 350g/12oz butternut squash, halved, seeded and cubed
2 courgettes, cubed
1 onion, chopped
1 red pepper, seeded and cut into small pieces
4 thyme sprigs, leaves removed
2 tbsp oil
4 boneless skinless chicken breasts, cut into bite-sized pieces
juice of 1 lemon
4 tbsp pesto
16 cherry tomatoes
400g/14oz dried penne pasta

Takes 1 hour • Serves 4

1 Preheat oven to 200°C/fan 180°C/gas 6. Put all the vegetables into a large roasting tin, scatter with the thyme and season. Drizzle with 2 tablespoons of the oil and roast for 40 minutes, turning halfway through.
2 Meanwhile, leave 8 wooden skewers to soak in water. Put the chicken into a shallow dish and mix with the lemon juice and pesto.
3 Thread the chicken pieces and whole tomatoes on to the skewers, then put them on a baking sheet. Drizzle with the rest of the olive oil and roast for 20 minutes, turning once, until the chicken is cooked through. Cook the pasta according to the packet instructions.
4 Toss the roasted vegetables and pasta together and serve with the pesto chicken kebabs.

• Per serving 668 kcalories, protein 51.8g, carbohydrate 90.6g, fat 13.5g, saturated fat 3.1g, fibre 6.5g, sugar 12.6g, salt 0.45g

Follow these simple steps to make a classic lunch or supper dish for all the family.

Macaroni cheese

700ml/1¼ pint full-fat milk
1 onion, peeled and halved
1 garlic clove, peeled
1 bay leaf (optional)
350g/12oz macaroni
50g/2oz butter, plus extra for greasing
50g/2oz plain flour
175g/6oz mature cheddar, grated
1 tsp English mustard powder or mustard
50g/2oz parmesan or more cheddar, grated
50g/2oz coarse white breadcrumbs

Takes 45 minutes, plus infusing
Serves 4

1 In a small pan, warm the milk with the onion, garlic and bay leaf (if using) until almost boiling. Remove from the heat, leave to infuse for 10 minutes, then strain.

2 Cook the macaroni according to the packet instructions. Drain, then rinse under the tap. Preheat oven to 190°C/fan 170°C/gas 5 and butter a large ovenproof dish. Melt the butter in a medium-sized pan. When foaming, add the flour, then cook, stirring constantly, for 1 minute on a low heat.

3 Slowly stir the infused milk into the flour mix until smooth. Simmer for 3–4 minutes, stirring often, until the sauce has thickened. Take off the heat, then add the 175g of cheddar, the mustard powder or mustard, season then stir.

4 Stir in the pasta, then tip into the baking dish. Sprinkle over the parmesan or cheddar and breadcrumbs, then bake for 15–20 minutes until golden and bubbling.

• Per serving 860 kcalories, protein 36g, carbohydrate 97g, fat 40g, saturated fat 24g, fibre 4g, sugar 13g, salt 1.72g

Pork meatballs make a welcome change to beef – and they cost less to make, too.

Fruity pork meatballs

300g pack pork mince
1 small onion, chopped
1 tsp mixed herbs
3 tbsp caramelized onion marmalade or onion chutney
300ml/½ pint hot vegetable stock
2 red apples, cored and thickly sliced
mash or jacket potatoes, to serve

Takes 20–25 minutes • Serves 4

1 Combine the mince, onion and herbs. Wet your hands and divide the mixture into 16 balls. Heat a large, non-stick frying pan, then brown the meatballs for 2 minutes over a high heat.

2 Stir in the onion marmalade, stock and apples, then bring to the boil. Simmer for about 15 minutes until the apples and pork are cooked and the sauce has thickened. Spoon the meatballs and sauce over mash or a jacket potato.

• Per serving 235 kcalories, protein 11g, carbohydrate 19g, fat 13g, saturated fat 6g, fibre 3g, sugar 13g, salt 1.54g

Toad in the hole is a classic money-saving recipe, the cheap-to-make batter making sausages go further. The trick to a good rise is to get the pan really hot before you add the batter.

Toad in the hole with onion gravy

100g/4oz plain flour, plus 1 tbsp for gravy
½ tsp English mustard powder
1 egg
300ml/½ pint milk
3 thyme sprigs, leaves only
8 plain pork sausages
2 tbsp sunflower oil
2 onions, peeled and sliced
500ml/18fl oz beef stock

Takes 1 hour • Serves 4

1 Preheat oven to 220°C/fan 200°C/gas 7. Mix together the flour, mustard powder and a good pinch of salt in a large bowl. Make a well in the flour and crack the egg into it, then pour in 100ml of the milk. Stir slowly to make a smooth batter – beating out any lumps. Stir in the remaining milk and the thyme leaves.
2 Tip the sausages into a 20cm x 30cm roasting tin. Add 1 tablespoon of the oil, tossing the sausages in it thoroughly to coat the base, then roast for 15 minutes.
3 Quickly pour the batter into the hot tin. Bake for 40 minutes until the batter is cooked through, well risen and crisp at the edges.
4 In a pan, cook the onions in the remaining oil over a medium heat for 20 minutes until golden brown. Add the remaining flour, then cook, stirring, for 2 minutes. Gradually stir in the stock to make a smooth gravy. Bubble to thicken, then season and serve with the toad in the hole.

• Per serving 520 kcalories, protein 25g, carbohydrate 37g, fat 31g, saturated fat 9g, fibre 2g, sugar 11g, salt 2.22g

If you haven't made lamb meatballs before, experiment with this tasty pilaf. For an even healthier version, substitute the lamb for turkey mince – it's a good source of protein and low in saturated fat.

Lamb meatball and pea pilaf

400g pack lean minced lamb
3 garlic cloves, crushed
2 tsp ground cumin
300g/10oz basmati rice
enough lamb or vegetable stock to
cover the rice (from a cube is fine)
300g/10oz frozen peas
zest of 2 lemons, juice of 1

FOR THE CUCUMBER YOGURT
½ cucumber, finely chopped
or grated
150g pot mild natural yogurt
small bunch of mint, leaves torn

Takes 30 minutes • Serves 4

1 Mix the lamb with half the garlic and 1 teaspoon of the cumin, then season and shape into about 16 balls (it's easier to do if you wet your hands). Heat a large frying pan then fry the meatballs for about 8 minutes until golden and cooked through. Remove from the pan, set aside, then tip in the rice and the remaining cumin and garlic. Fry for 30 seconds, stirring, then pour in enough stock to cover. Cover and simmer for 10 minutes or until almost all of the liquid is absorbed.
2 Stir in the peas, return the meatballs to the pan, then warm through for a few minutes until the peas are tender. Meanwhile, mix the cucumber, yogurt and half the mint together, then season. To finish the pilaf, stir in the lemon zest and juice with some seasoning and the remaining mint. Serve with a good dollop of the cooling cucumber yogurt.

• Per serving 496 kcalories, protein 33g, carbohydrate 72g, fat 10g, saturated fat 4g, fibre 4g, sugar 5g, salt 1.34g

Using the meat from good-quality sausages is an easy way to get lots of flavour into mince dishes without having to add extra herbs, spices and seasoning.

Quick sausage bolognese

6 good-quality sausages, skins removed
1 tsp fennel seeds (optional)
250g pack mushrooms, sliced
150ml/¼ pint red wine (optional)
660g jar tomato pasta sauce
300g/10oz penne or other pasta shapes
grated or shaved parmesan, to serve (optional)

Takes 20 minutes • Serves 4

1 Heat a large, wide frying pan, then crumble in the sausage meat and fennel seeds (there's no need to add any oil). Fry for a few minutes until golden and the fat is released, stirring well to break up the meat. Add the mushrooms and fry for a few minutes until beginning to soften. Stir in the wine, if using, bubble for 1 minute, then add the tomato sauce and heat through until bubbling.
2 Meanwhile, cook the pasta according to the packet instructions. When ready, drain and tip into the sauce. Mix well until completely coated, then divide among four plates, sprinkling with a little parmesan, if you like, before serving.

• Per serving 657 kcalories, protein 27g, carbohydrate 75g, fat 30g, saturated fat 8g, fibre 5g, sugar 15g, salt 2.98g

Cooked slowly, stewing cuts simmer into melting tenderness and give far more flavour than any quick-cook steaks or expensive joints.

Herby lamb cobbler

1 tbsp sunflower oil
200g/8oz smoked streaky bacon, chopped
900g/2lb stewing lamb, cut into large chunks
350g/12oz baby onions, peeled
5 carrots, cut into large chunks
350g/12oz button mushrooms
3 tbsp plain flour
3 bay leaves
small bunch of thyme
350ml/12fl oz red wine
350ml/12fl oz lamb or beef stock
large splash of Worcestershire sauce

FOR THE COBBLER TOPPING
350g/12oz self-raising flour
4 tbsp chopped mixed herbs, including thyme, rosemary and parsley
200g/8oz chilled butter, cubed
juice of 1 lemon
5 bay leaves
1 beaten egg, to glaze

Takes about 3 hours • Serves 6

1 Preheat oven to 180°C/fan 160°C/gas 4. In a flameproof casserole, heat the oil, then sizzle the bacon for 5 minutes. Turn up the heat, then brown the lamb in batches. Remove with a slotted spoon. Fry the onions, carrots and mushrooms for 5 minutes, then stir in the flour. Return the meat to the pan with the herbs, wine, stock and Worcestershire sauce. Season, cover and braise for 1 hour 20 minutes.
2 Make the topping just before the lamb's cooking time is up. Tip the flour, herbs and seasoning into a large bowl. Rub in the butter. Make a well, then add the lemon juice and 3 tablespoons of water. Bring together to form a soft dough. Roll out to about 5mm thick, then cut into rounds with a 7cm cutter, re-rolling any trimmings. Overlap the circles of dough and bay leaves on the top of the stew. Brush with egg and bake for 45 minutes until golden.

• Per serving 963 kcalories, protein 45g, carbohydrate 59g, fat 60g, saturated fat 31g, fibre 5g, sugar 9g, salt 2.89g

Feed the family for less

A classic family recipe that the kids will love. Serve with your favourite green veg for a complete meal.

Tasty cottage pies

FOR THE FILLING
2 onions, sliced
2 tbsp olive oil
500g/1lb 2oz lean minced beef
2 beef stock cubes
3 tbsp brown sauce
415g can reduced sugar and salt baked beans

FOR THE TOPPING
900g/2lb large potatoes, quartered
3 medium carrots, thickly sliced
25g/1oz butter
a good splash of milk
40g/1½oz mature cheddar, grated
4 small tomatoes, quartered
broccoli florets or peas, to serve

Takes 1½ hours • Serves 4

1 Preheat oven to 200°C/fan 180°C/gas 6. Fry the onions in the oil for 5 minutes until soft and golden. Add the mince, breaking it up well, and fry until it has browned. Add a mug of water, the stock cubes and brown sauce. Cover and simmer over a low heat for 10 minutes, stirring every now and then.
2 Boil the potatoes and carrots together in salted water for 15 minutes or until tender. Drain and return to the pan with the butter and milk, then mash until smooth with an electric whisk or potato masher.
3 Stir the beans into the meat mix, simmer for 2 minutes, then spoon into 4 mini pie dishes. Spoon the mash over the top. Put the pie dishes on a baking sheet and top with the cheese and the tomatoes. Bake for 35 minutes or until the tops are golden. Serve with broccoli or peas.

• Per serving 634 kcalories, protein 42g, carbohydrate 57g, fat 28g, saturated fat 12g, fibre 9g, sugar 15g, salt 3.65g

You can't beat sausage casserole – it's comfort food at its best.

Sausage casserole with garlic toasts

8 reduced-fat sausages
1 yellow pepper, seeded and chopped
4 red onions, cut into wedges
400g can chopped tomatoes
250ml/9fl oz hot vegetable stock
1 tbsp sugar
½ × 20g pack basil

FOR THE TOASTS
400g/14oz bloomer loaf
25g/1oz low-fat soft cheese
1 tbsp butter
2 garlic cloves, crushed
½ × 20g pack basil, chopped

Takes 45 minutes • Serves 4

1 Preheat oven to 220°C/fan 200°C/gas 7. Put the sausages, pepper and onions into a roasting tin, then roast for 20 minutes.
2 Lower the oven to 200°C/fan 180°C/gas 6, then tip the tomatoes and stock over the sausages. Add the sugar and most of the basil season, then stir well. Roast for another 20 minutes.
3 To make the toasts, lightly toast the bread on both sides. Mix together the cheese, butter, garlic and chopped basil then spread one side of the toast with this herby mix and grill briefly until melted and golden.
4 Serve the garlic toasts with the sausage casserole, sprinkled with the remaining basil.

• Per serving (with toasts) 568 kcalories, protein 28g, carbohydrate 78g, fat 18g, saturated fat 7g, fibre 6g, sugar 19g, salt 4.24g

Canned beans take on masses of flavour in this French-style dish. To make it that bit more special, chuck in a glass of wine with the stock.

Braised chicken and beans

2 tbsp olive oil
8 boneless skinless chicken thighs
2 onions, chopped
2 garlic cloves, chopped
1 tsp dried thyme
600ml/1 pint chicken or vegetable stock
2 × 400g cans flageolet, cannellini or butter beans
a handful of parsley leaves

Takes 1 hour • Serves 4

1 Heat the oil in a large frying pan with a lid, add the chicken, then quickly brown it all over. Tip in the onions, garlic and thyme, then fry for a further 2 minutes. Pour in the stock, 150ml of water and a little salt and pepper. Bring to the boil, then simmer for 40 minutes, covering halfway through the cooking time, until the chicken is tender.
2 Stir the beans into the pan and briefly warm through. Roughly chop the parsley, then scatter over to serve.

• Per serving 444 kcalories, protein 54.4g, carbohydrate 29g, fat 13.2g, saturated fat 2.7g, fibre 8.2g, sugar 6.9g, salt 2.48g

Don't just save Thai for a takeaway – once you've made your own fragrant curry you'll be hooked on home-made.

Easy Thai prawn curry

1 tbsp vegetable oil
1 onion, chopped
1 tsp grated fresh root ginger
1–2 tsp Thai red curry paste
400g can chopped tomatoes
50g sachet coconut cream
400g/14oz cooked frozen prawns
plain rice and chopped coriander
leaves, to serve (optional)

Takes 20 minutes • Serves 4

1 Heat the oil in a medium pan. Tip in the onion and ginger, then cook for a few minutes until softened. Stir in the curry paste and cook for 1 minute more. Pour over the chopped tomatoes and coconut cream. Bring to the boil, then leave to simmer for 10 minutes, adding a little boiling water if the mixture gets too thick.
2 Tip in the prawns, then cook for 5 minutes more, until heated through. Serve with plain rice and sprinkled with a little chopped coriander, if you like.

• Per serving 180 kcalories, protein 20g, carbohydrate 6g, fat 9g, saturated fat 4g, fibre 1g, sugar 5g, salt 0.86g

You'll love the fresh flavour of this sauce. Adapt it with chillies, mushrooms, bacon, anchovies or olives – the choice is yours.

Simple pasta with tomato and basil sauce

400g/14oz pasta
1 tbsp olive oil
1 garlic clove, crushed
400g can chopped tomatoes
1 tsp vegetable stock powder or
½ crumbled stock cube
1 tbsp tomato purée
1 tsp sugar
a few basil leaves

Takes 20 minutes • Serves 4

1 Boil the pasta according to the packet instructions.
2 Heat the oil in a pan, add the garlic, then gently fry for 1 minute. Tip in all the other ingredients, except the basil, and bring to the boil. Reduce the heat, then simmer uncovered for 5 minutes, stirring occasionally. To finish, roughly tear the basil leaves and stir them into the sauce.
3 Drain the pasta, reserving a little of the cooking water. Stir the pasta and reserved water into the sauce and serve.

• Per serving 394 kcalories, protein 13.6g, carbohydrate 79g, fat 4.8g, saturated fat 0.7g, fibre 4.1g, sugar 7.5g, salt 0.29g

Fish is a healthy choice for the whole family. This tasty twist on fish and mushy peas is high in omega 3 and counts as two of your 5-a-day.

Lemon fish with basil bean mash

4 small bunches of cherry tomatoes on the vine
1 tbsp olive oil
4 × 140g/5oz chunks white fish fillet (frozen is good value)
zest of 1 lemon, plus juice of ½
480g pack frozen soya beans
2 garlic cloves
bunch of basil, leaves and stalks separated
200ml/7fl oz chicken or vegetable stock

Takes 25 minutes • Serves 4

1 Preheat oven to 200°C/fan 180°C/gas 6. Put the tomatoes on to a baking sheet, rub with a little of the oil and some seasoning, then roast for 5 minutes until the skins are starting to split. Add the fish, top with most of the lemon zest and some more seasoning, then drizzle with a little more oil. Roast for 8–10 minutes until the fish flakes easily.
2 Meanwhile, cook the beans in a pan of boiling water for 3 minutes until just tender. Drain, then tip into a food processor with the remaining oil, the garlic, basil stalks, lemon juice and stock, then pulse to a thick, slightly rough purée. Season to taste.
3 Divide the tomatoes and bean mash among four plates, top with the fish, then scatter with basil leaves and the remaining lemon zest to serve.

• Per serving 372 kcalories, protein 44g, carbohydrate 17g, fat 15g, saturated fat 3g, fibre 6g, sugar 3g, salt 0.5g

Gnocchi is a delicious change from pasta and potatoes. It's available in most supermarkets and makes a filling family meal.

Gnocchi and tomato bake

1 tbsp olive oil
1 onion, chopped
1 red pepper, seeded and finely chopped
1 garlic clove, crushed
400g can chopped tomatoes
500g pack gnocchi
a handful of basil leaves, torn
½ × 125g ball mozzarella, torn into chunks

Takes 30 minutes • Serves 4

1 Heat grill to High. Heat the oil in a large frying pan, then soften the onion and pepper for 5 minutes. Stir in the garlic, fry for 1 minute, then tip in the tomatoes and gnocchi and bring to a simmer. Bubble for 10–15 minutes, stirring occasionally, until the gnocchi is soft and the sauce has thickened. Season, stir through the basil, then transfer to a large ovenproof dish.
2 Scatter with the mozzarella and grill for 5–6 minutes until the cheese is bubbling and golden.

• Per serving 285 kcalories, protein 10g, carbohydrate 50g, fat 7g, saturated fat 3g, fibre 4g, sugar 8g, salt 1.64g

Add a little Spanish spice to chicken with a little chorizo. The sausage bastes the chicken as it roasts and gives the whole dish a deliciously garlicky paprika flavour.

Chorizo chicken with chilli wedges

4 large sweet potatoes, peeled and cut into wedges
1 tsp olive oil
1 tsp dried chilli flakes
12 thin chorizo slices
4 boneless skinless chicken breasts
a few thyme sprigs, leaves stripped, or 1 tsp dried thyme

Takes 35 minutes • Serves 4

1 Preheat oven to 220°C/fan 200°C/gas 7. Put the sweet potatoes on a large baking sheet, then toss with the oil and chilli flakes, and season. Roast for 10 minutes, then remove and reduce the oven temperature to 200°C/fan 180°C/gas 6.

2 Lay 3 slices of chorizo over each chicken breast, and secure with a cocktail stick. Lift the chicken on to the baking sheet next to the potato wedges. Scatter the wedges with thyme leaves, then roast for another 20 minutes until the chicken is golden, turning them halfway through cooking.

• Per serving 422 kcalories, protein 39g, carbohydrate 54g, fat 7g, saturated fat 2g, fibre 6g, sugar 15g, salt 0.66g

Barbecue sauce is dead easy to make yourself and tastes fabulous with pork and juicy buttered corn.

BBQ pork steaks with smoky corn

4 tbsp tomato ketchup
2 tbsp dark muscovado sugar
1 tbsp white wine vinegar
1 tsp paprika
4 pork loin steaks, trimmed of any fat
4 corn cobs
1 tbsp butter
green salad, to serve

Takes 20 minutes • Serves 4

1 Boil a large pan of water for the corn and make the sauce by mixing together the ketchup, sugar and vinegar with half the paprika.

2 Heat a non-stick frying pan, then brown the pork for 3–4 minutes on each side. Spoon over the sauce halfway through cooking and turn the steaks in it until the pork is cooked through and sticky.

3 Meanwhile, tip the corn into the boiling water and cook for 5–8 minutes until tender. Stir the remaining paprika into the butter in a heatproof bowl and microwave on High for 15–20 seconds until the paprika is sizzling in the melted butter (alternatively, just melt the smoky butter in a small pan). Drain the corn, brush over the butter, then serve with the sticky pork steaks and a green salad.

• Per serving 320 kcalories, protein 30g, carbohydrate 30g, fat 10g, saturated fat 4g, fibre 2g, sugar 14g, salt 0.88g

Here's proof that creamy curries don't have to be bad for your waistline. Serve with basmati rice and scattered with coriander and almonds.

Creamy aubergine curry

2 onions, roughly chopped
4cm piece fresh root ginger, chopped
4 tbsp toasted flaked almonds, plus 1 tbsp to serve
1 tbsp curry powder
small bunch of coriander, stalks and leaves separated
2 tsp olive oil
2 aubergines, chopped into large wedges
200g pot thick Greek yogurt
400ml/14oz hot water
basmati rice, to serve

Takes 30 minutes • Serves 4

1 Whiz the onions, ginger, almonds, curry powder and coriander stalks in a mini food processor until pulpy (add a splash of water if needed). Boil a kettle full of water.
2 Heat the oil in a pan, then fry the aubergines for 5 minutes until browned. Scoop them out using a slotted spoon and set aside. Add the onion paste to the pan and cook for a few minutes, stirring, until the onions soften. Return the aubergine to the pan with the yogurt and the hot water. Stir, then simmer for 10–15 minutes until the aubergine is tender. Season well, scatter with extra almonds and the chopped coriander leaves and serve with basmati rice.

• Per serving 190 kcalories, protein 8g, carbohydrate 11g, fat 13g, saturated fat 4g, fibre 6g, sugar 8g, salt 0.15g

Roast some potato wedges and heat up some baked beans to go with this easy breakfast-come-dinner dish.

All-in-one baked mushrooms

2 tbsp olive oil
4 very large field mushrooms
4 slices good-quality cooked ham
4 eggs

Takes 30 minutes • Serves 2
(easily doubled)

1 Preheat oven to 220°C/fan 200°C/gas 7. Drizzle a little olive oil over the base of a ceramic baking dish, then pop in the mushrooms. Drizzle with the remaining oil and season. Bake for 15 minutes until soft, then remove from the oven.
2 Tuck the ham slices around the mushrooms to create little pockets. Crack the eggs into the pockets, then return to the oven for 10 minutes until the egg white is set and the yolk is still a little runny. Serve scooped straight from the dish.

• Per serving 379 kcalories, protein 30g, carbohydrate 1g, fat 28g, saturated fat 6g, fibre 3g, sugar 1g, salt 1.79g

A little chorizo transforms some very ordinary storecupboard ingredients into a main meal you'll make again and again!

Paella fried rice

300g/10oz basmati rice
1 tbsp vegetable oil
2 small chorizo sausages, sliced
1 onion, sliced
1 garlic clove, chopped
½ tsp turmeric
200g/8oz frozen cooked prawns
100g/4oz frozen peas
150ml/¼ pint boiling water
lemon wedges, to serve

Takes 35 minutes • Serves 4

1 Rinse the rice until the water runs clear, tip into a pan, cover with cold water to a fingertip's depth and bring to the boil. Season, then cover and simmer for 10 minutes or until all of the liquid has been absorbed, then take off the heat and let it rest for 10 minutes. Fluff up with a fork.
2 Heat the oil in a frying pan. Tip in the chorizo, onion and garlic, then cook for a couple of minutes until softened. Stir through the turmeric, followed by the rice, prawns and peas and the boiling water. Keep stirring until everything is warmed through. Serve with lemon wedges.

• Per serving 347 kcalories, protein 20g, carbohydrate 50g, fat 9g, saturated fat 2g, fibre 2g, sugar 3g, salt 1.19g

Making pizza doesn't take much longer than ordering one in – and it's good fun for kids too.

Perfect pizza

FOR THE BASE
300g/10oz strong bread flour, plus extra for kneading
1 tsp fast-action yeast
1 tsp salt
200ml/7fl oz warm water
1 tbsp olive oil, plus extra for drizzling
125g ball mozzarella, sliced
handful of grated cheddar or parmesan
handful of cherry tomatoes, halved

FOR THE TOMATO SAUCE
100ml/3½fl oz passata
a handful of fresh basil or 1 tsp dried, plus extra leaves to serve (optional)
1 garlic clove, crushed

Takes 30 minutes • Serves 4 (makes 2 pizzas)

1 Combine the flour, yeast and salt in a bowl. Make a well, pour in the warm water and the olive oil, and mix well. Turn on to a lightly floured surface and knead for 5 minutes until smooth. There's no need to let it rise.

2 Mix together the passata, basil and garlic for the sauce, then season.

3 On a floured surface, roll out the dough into two large thin rounds about 25cm across. Lift on to floured baking sheets. Preheat oven to 240°C/fan 220°C /gas 9. Put another baking sheet or an upturned baking sheet in the oven on the top shelf.

4 Smooth the sauce over the bases, scatter with the cheese and tomatoes, drizzle with oil and season. Bake on top of the preheated baking sheet for 8–10 minutes until crisp. Serve with a little more olive oil and basil leaves, if using.

• Per serving 431 kcalories, protein 19g, carbohydrate 59g, fat 15g, saturated fat 7g, fibre 3g, sugar 2g, salt 1.87g

If your family like shepherd's pie, they'll love these special baked spuds. You could make these the night before, then simply bake them for 20 minutes when you get in.

Shepherd's pie potatoes

2 tbsp butter
1 large onion, chopped
500g pack lean minced beef
500ml/14fl oz hot beef stock
1 tbsp Worcestershire sauce
2 tbsp tomato purée
4 large jacket potatoes, baked or microwaved
2 good handfuls of grated cheddar
your favourite veg, to serve

Takes 1 hour • Serves 4

1 Preheat oven to 200°C/fan 180°C/gas 6. Melt half the butter in a non-stick pan. Cook the onion for 3–4 minutes, then increase the heat and add the mince. Fry for a further 3–4 minutes until the beef has browned. Stir in the stock, Worcestershire sauce, tomato purée and some seasoning. Gently bubble for 15–20 minutes until the mince is tender and the sauce has thickened.
2 To assemble, cut the jacket potatoes in half lengthways and scoop the flesh into a small bowl, leaving the skin intact. Mash the potato with the remaining butter and season well. Divide the mince among the potato skins, then cover with the mash. Transfer the potatoes to a baking dish, sprinkle with cheese, then bake for 20 minutes until golden. Serve with your favourite veg.

• Per serving 779 kcalories, protein 50g, carbohydrate 79g, fat 31g, saturated fat 15g, fibre 7g, sugar 9g, salt 2.43g

Good-for-you baked beans that are cheap but taste brilliant. The wedges are a complete winner – they go with so many meals.

Better-than-baked beans with spicy wedges

1 tsp oil
1 onion, halved and thinly sliced
2 rashers streaky bacon, cut into large-ish pieces
1 tsp sugar (brown, if you have it)
400g can chopped tomatoes
200ml/7fl oz vegetable stock (from a cube)
410g can cannellini, butter or haricot beans in water

FOR THE WEDGES
1 tbsp white flour (plain or self-raising)
½ tsp cayenne, paprika or mild chilli powder
1 tsp dried mixed herbs (optional)
2 baking potatoes, each cut into 8 wedges
2 tsp oil

Takes 45 minutes • Serves 2 (easily doubled)

1 Preheat oven to 200°C/fan 180°C/gas 6. For the wedges, mix the flour, cayenne and herbs (if using), add some salt and pepper, then toss with the potatoes and oil until well coated. Tip into a roasting tin, then bake for about 35 minutes until crisp and cooked through.

2 Meanwhile, heat the oil in a non-stick pan, then gently fry the onion and bacon together for 5–10 minutes until the onions are softened and just starting to turn golden. Stir in the sugar, tomatoes, stock and seasoning to taste, then simmer the sauce for 5 minutes. Add the beans, then simmer for another 5 minutes until the sauce has thickened. Serve with the wedges.

• Per serving 399 kcalories, protein 19g, carbohydrate 60g, fat 11g, saturated fat 2g, fibre 12g, sugar 15g, salt 1.14g

Tagines are a type of classic Moroccan stew – just perfect for serving with a steaming mound of couscous or over crisp jacket potatoes.

Tasty veg tagine

4 carrots, cut into chunks
4 small parsnips or 3 large, cut into chunks
3 red onions, cut into wedges
2 red peppers, seeded and cut into chunks
2 tbsp olive oil
1 tsp each ground cumin, paprika, cinnamon and mild chilli powder
400g can chopped tomatoes
2 small handfuls of soft dried apricots
2 tsp clear honey
couscous or jacket potatoes, to serve

Takes 45 minutes • Serves 4

1 Preheat oven to 200°C/fan 180°C/gas 6. Scatter the veg over a couple of baking sheets, drizzle with half the oil, season, then, using your hands, rub the oil over the veg to coat. Roast for 30 minutes until tender and beginning to brown.
2 Meanwhile, in a frying pan, cook the spices in the remaining oil for 1 minute – they should sizzle and start to smell aromatic. Tip in the tomatoes, apricots, honey and a can of water. Simmer for 5 minutes until the sauce is slightly reduced and the apricots plump, then stir in the veg and some seasoning. Serve with couscous or jacket potatoes.

• Per serving 272 kcalories, protein 7g, carbohydrate 45g, fat 8g, saturated fat 1g, fibre 12g, sugar 32g, salt 0.35g

With stand-bys in your cupboard, you can make a stir fry quickly and cheaply. For even better value, switch the chicken for turkey.

Sticky chicken stir fry with sesame seeds

175g/6oz egg noodles
2 tsp sunflower oil
2 chicken breasts, sliced into strips
3 carrots, cut into matchsticks
2 tbsp clear honey
1 tbsp soy sauce
juice of 2 limes
3 tbsp sesame seeds, toasted
a small bunch of coriander, roughly chopped

Takes 20 minutes • Serves 2

1 Cook the noodles according to the packet instructions, then drain and toss with 1 teaspoon of the oil to stop them sticking together.
2 Meanwhile, heat the remaining teaspoon of oil in a large wok, add the chicken, then stir-fry over a high heat for a few minutes. Tip in the carrot sticks, then continue stir-frying for about 4 minutes until the chicken is cooked and starting to brown.
3 Quickly stir in the honey, soy sauce and lime juice, allow to bubble for 30 seconds, then add the sesame seeds and cooked noodles. (At this stage it's easier to use tongs to mix everything together.) Warm everything through briefly, then toss in the coriander just before serving.

• Per serving 799 kcalories, protein 53.4g, carbohydrate 110.9g, fat 18.9g, saturated fat 2.7g, fibre 7.9g, sugar 25g, salt 3.42g

Home-made fish fingers are quick to prepare, good for you and convenient – you can even cook them from frozen. Try great-value pollack as a sustainable and tasty alternative to cod.

Crunchy fish fingers

250g/9oz pollack fillets
juice of ½ lemon
½ tsp fish seasoning (we used Schwartz)
50g/2oz polenta
50g/2oz dried breadcrumbs
1 egg, lightly beaten
2 tbsp olive oil, to drizzle
your favourite veg, to serve

Takes 25 minutes • Serves 4

1 Preheat oven to 200°C/fan 180°C/gas 6. Cut the fish into 8 pieces, then squeeze over the lemon juice.
2 Mix the fish seasoning, polenta and breadcrumbs on a plate. Dip the fish into the beaten egg, then turn several times in the polenta and breadcrumb mixture to coat. Repeat with all the pieces of fish, then put on a baking sheet lined with non-stick baking paper.
3 Drizzle the fish fingers with olive oil and bake for 15 minutes, turning halfway through cooking. Serve with your favourite veg.

• Per serving 205 kcalories, protein 15g, carbohydrate 20g, fat 8g, saturated fat 1g, fibre none, sugar 1g, salt 0.32g

Indian spices and eggs work together brilliantly in this filling veggie meal.

Spiced tortilla

1 tbsp sunflower oil
1 onion, sliced
1 red chilli, seeded and shredded
2 tsp curry spices (we mixed coriander, cumin and turmeric)
300g/10oz cherry tomatoes
500g/1lb 2oz cooked potatoes, sliced
bunch of coriander, stalks finely chopped, leaves roughly chopped
8 eggs, beaten
green salad, to serve

Takes 25 minutes • Serves 4

1 Heat the oil in a large frying pan. Fry the onion and half the chilli for 5 minutes until softened. Tip in the curry spices, fry for 1 minute more, then add the cherry tomatoes, potatoes and coriander stalks to the pan. Season the eggs well, pour over the top of the veg and leave to cook gently for 8–10 minutes until almost set.
2 Heat the grill and flash the tortilla underneath it for 1–2 minutes until the top is set. Scatter the coriander leaves and remaining chilli over the top, slice into wedges and serve with a green salad.

• Per serving 327 kcalories, protein 19g, carbohydrate 27g, fat 17g, saturated fat 4g, fibre 3g, sugar 5g, salt 0.69g

Risottos are so comforting to eat and relaxing to make – and won't break your budget.

Mushroom, chicken and bacon risotto

8 rashers smoked streaky bacon, chopped
50g/2oz butter
1 onion, finely chopped
250g pack mushrooms, sliced
300g/10oz risotto rice
1 small glass of white wine
1.5litres/2¾ pints hot chicken stock
about 200g cooked chicken, skinned and chopped (ideally leftover roast chicken)
a handful of parsley leaves, chopped
50g/2oz parmesan, finely grated

Takes 30 minutes • Serves 4

1 Fry the bacon in half the butter, then add the onion. Once soft, add the mushrooms and cook for 3 minutes more. Stir in the rice until it's coated in the butter, then stir continuously until the edges of the grains start to look transparent.

2 Pour in the wine and simmer until totally evaporated. Reduce the heat then add the stock, a ladleful at a time, stirring with each addition until absorbed. This will take 25–30 minutes. The rice should be just cooked and the risotto should be creamy and slightly soupy.

3 When you add the final ladle of stock, stir through the chicken pieces to reheat them. Add the chopped parsley with the parmesan and remaining butter, leave to rest off the heat for a few minutes, then stir through and serve.

• Per serving 785 kcalories, protein 56g, carbohydrate 68g, fat 33g, saturated fat 14g, fibre 5g, sugar 5g, salt 3.69g

A fabulous tart that's perfect as a starter or light lunch. Curd cheese is a soft, very creamy cheese, available at most deli counters. You could use cream cheese or mascarpone instead.

Tomato and curd cheese tart

200g/8oz plain flour, plus extra for dusting
100g/4oz butter, cold and cubed
50g/2oz mature cheddar, grated
small bunch of basil, leaves roughly chopped
175g/6oz curd cheese
8 ripe medium tomatoes, thinly sliced
a little olive oil, to drizzle and serve
a handful of mixed soft herbs (we used chervil, mint, and flat-leaf parsley), to garnish

Takes 1½ hours • Serves 8

1 Put the flour, ½ teaspoon salt and the butter into a food processor and blend until roughly mixed. Tip into a bowl, stir in two-thirds of the cheddar, then 100ml of ice-cold water. Knead quickly, then chill the pastry for 30 minutes. In a bowl, mix together the basil, the remaining cheddar and the curd cheese, then season.
2 Roll the pastry out to a long rectangle. Fold the top third down, then the bottom third up. Repeat 3 times. Chill for another 10 minutes.
3 Preheat oven to 220°C/fan 200°C/gas 7. Roll out the pastry again until large enough to cut a circle about the size of a dinner plate. Place on a floured baking sheet, prick all over with a fork, then bake for 15 minutes. Cool, then spread over the herby cheese mix, almost to the edge. Lay the tomatoes on top, overlapping.
4 Season and bake for 15 minutes. Turn down to 150°C/fan 130°C/gas 2 and bake for 40 minutes. Cool a little, then drizzle with oil. Toss the herbs with more oil, then pile on to the tart to serve.

• Per serving 278 kcalories, protein 8g, carbohydrate 24g, fat 17g, saturated fat 10g, fibre 2g, sugar 4g, salt 0.58g

Feeding a crowd needn't cost a bomb. All this tasty one-pot needs to accompany it is some good crusty bread and simple steamed greens.

Chicken with bacon and butter beans

1 tbsp olive oil
6 chicken legs, skin on
200g/8oz streaky bacon, chopped
4 red onions, cut into wedges
2 garlic cloves, crushed
2 rosemary sprigs, leaves finely chopped, plus 1 whole sprig
250ml/9fl oz red wine
250ml/9fl oz chicken stock
2 × 400g cans cherry tomatoes
3 × 400g cans butter beans in water, drained
2 tbsp sugar
1 bay leaf
steamed greens and crusty bread, to serve

Takes 1¼ hours • Serves 6

1 Preheat oven to 190°C/fan 170°C/gas 5. Heat the oil in a large roasting tin, then brown the chicken legs in batches until golden and crisp. Remove from the tin and set aside.
2 Sizzle the bacon in the same tin until just golden then add the onions, garlic and chopped rosemary. Fry for a few minutes, stirring, then pour in the wine and stock. Bring to the boil, then simmer for 10 minutes until the onions are starting to soften and the liquid has reduced. Tip in the tomatoes, beans, sugar, bay leaf, remaining sprig of rosemary and seasoning. Stir, then bring back to a simmer.
3 Sit the chicken legs on top of the bean mix. Bake for 40–45 minutes until the chicken is cooked and crisp, the sauce is bubbling and the onions are soft.

• Per serving 701 kcalories, protein 55g, carbohydrate 30g, fat 39g, saturated fat 12g, fibre 7g, sugar 14g, salt 2.82g

Pâtés and parfaits are the ultimate in economical entertaining, as they cost little but taste fabulous. Serve with toast, chutney and gherkins.

Velvety liver parfait

250g pack butter, diced and slightly softened
2 shallots, finely sliced
1 garlic clove, sliced
600g/1lb 5oz chicken livers, any sinews cut away
a good splash of brandy
1 tbsp tomato purée
toast, sliced gherkins and chutney, to serve

FOR THE TOPPING
100g/4oz butter
1 tbsp thyme leaves
1 tsp cracked black peppercorns

Takes 45 minutes, plus cooling
Serves 6 with leftovers

1 Heat about a third of the butter in a large frying pan, then gently fry the shallots and garlic for 3–4 minutes until soft. Turn up the heat, add the livers, then fry until just browned on all sides. Add the brandy then boil down – if the sauce catches light for an instant, all the better. Cool completely.

2 Season generously, then tip into a processor with the tomato purée and remaining butter and blitz until smooth. Push through a fine sieve, then tip into a serving dish and smooth the top. Chill for at least 4 hours until set.

3 For the topping, melt the butter then leave for a minute to separate. Scatter the thyme and peppercorns over the parfait, then pour the yellow layer of butter on top. Chill to set. Serve with plenty of toast, sliced gherkins and chutney. Will keep for 2 days in the fridge.

• Per serving 535 kcalories, protein 18g, carbohydrate 2g, fat 50g, saturated fat 31g, fibre none, sugar 1g, salt 1.11g

If you think you can't stretch to smoked salmon, think again. Packs of trimmings contain the same fish, only in smaller pieces. This salad goes brilliantly with prawns, too.

Smoked salmon with grapefruit salad

3 grapefruit (a selection of yellow and pink, if you like)
100ml/3½fl oz olive oil
1 lemon
12 slices smoked salmon
a large handful of coriander sprigs, to garnish
brown bread and butter, to serve (optional)

Takes 30 minutes • Serves 4

1 Peel the grapefruit then cut away the pith and cut into segments over a pan, to catch any juice. Put the segments on a plate to one side. Squeeze the juice out of the membrane you are left with as well. Boil the juice in the pan for about 10 minutes until reduced to a few syrupy tablespoons. Mix with the olive oil and set aside.

2 Peel the lemon and cut away the pith then segment and carefully mix with the grapefruit segments. Drape the smoked salmon over 4 plates and scatter with the fruit segments. Spoon over the dressing and garnish with the coriander sprigs. Delicious served with slices of brown bread and butter.

• Per serving 354 kcalories, protein 20g, carbohydrate 10g, fat 26g, saturated fat 4g, fibre 2g, sugar 10g, salt 3.6g

These look special but are incredibly simple to make, especially as the pastry is ready-rolled. Asparagus is an inexpensive luxury when in season.

Asparagus and parmesan pastries

6 tbsp mascarpone
40g/1½oz grated parmesan, plus shavings to serve
3 tbsp finely chopped basil
zest of ½ lemon
375g pack ready-rolled puff pastry, quartered, then cut to the length of the asparagus
350g pack asparagus spears
1 tbsp olive oil
a good handful of pretty salad leaves tossed in vinaigrette, to serve

Takes 35 minutes • Serves 4

1 Preheat oven to 200°C/fan 180°C/gas 6. Mix the mascarpone with the parmesan, basil and lemon zest, then season.
2 Lift the pastry on to 2 baking sheets, then score around the edges of each piece to make a thin border. Spread over the cheese mixture, within the borders.
3 Toss the asparagus in the oil, then arrange in bundles on top of the pastry (these can be stacked a bit for height). Bake the pastries for 20–25 minutes until golden. Serve warm topped with the dressed salad leaves and a few shavings of parmesan.

• Per serving 535 kcalories, protein 12g, carbohydrate 37g, fat 39g, saturated fat 18g, fibre 1g, sugar 4g, salt 0.99g

If you find the name of this cut off-putting, consider that, when cured and sliced, this is what we know as streaky bacon. Belly is the cheapest pork roasting joint; it's rich, so a little goes a long way.

Crisp Chinese pork

1.3kg/3lb piece boned pork belly, skin on and scored (ask the butcher for the thin end if you can)
2 tsp Chinese five spice powder
2 tsp sea salt
boiled rice and steamed greens, to serve (optional)

FOR THE DIPPING SAUCE
4 tbsp soy sauce
a small piece of fresh root ginger, grated
1 tbsp Thai sweet chilli sauce
1 spring onion, finely chopped

Takes 2 hours 10 minutes, plus salting
Serves 4

1 Rub the pork with the five spice and sea salt then leave, uncovered, in the fridge for at least 2 hours, but preferably overnight.
2 Preheat the oven to its maximum setting then lay the pork on a rack over a roasting tin, making sure the skin is exposed. Roast for 10 minutes before turning down the heat to 180°C/fan 160°C/gas 4, then leave to cook for a further 1½ hours. Have a look at the pork; if the skin isn't crisp, turn up the heat to 220°C/fan 200°C/gas 7, then cook for another 30 minutes until it is. Remove from the oven and leave to rest on a board for at least 10 minutes before cutting.
3 To make the dipping sauce, mix all the ingredients together with 2 tablespoons of water. Cut the pork into small pieces, then serve with the sauce, plus boiled rice and steamed greens, if you like.

• Per serving 696 kcalories, protein 59g, carbohydrate 3g, fat 50g, saturated fat 19g, fibre none, sugar 2g, salt 5.83g

Just five ingredients meld into one delicious stew – that's clever entertaining. Serve with rice or couscous.

Moroccan lamb

500g/1lb 2oz lamb neck fillet, cut into bite-sized pieces
2 tsp paprika
3 tsp ground cinnamon
2 × 400g cans chopped tomatoes with olive oil and garlic
1 tbsp finely chopped parsley, plus extra to serve
rice or couscous, to serve

Takes 45 minutes • Serves 4

1 Heat a large, non-stick frying pan. Brown the lamb well on all sides without adding oil. Tip in the spices, then fry for 1 minute more until aromatic.
2 Tip in the chopped tomatoes and parsley, bring to the boil, then simmer gently, with a lid on, for 30 minutes or until the lamb is tender. Serve sprinkled with more parsley.

• Per serving 350 kcalories, protein 27g, carbohydrate 13g, fat 22g, saturated fat 9g, fibre 2g, sugar 9g, salt 1.47g

Not all soufflés are scary. Keep your cool in the kitchen and serve this sensational dish as an elegant wintry starter or lunch.

Make-ahead mushroom soufflés

140g/5oz button mushrooms, sliced
50g/2oz butter, plus extra for greasing
25g/1oz plain flour
325ml/11fl oz milk
85g/3oz gruyere, finely grated, plus a little extra for baking
3 eggs, separated
6 tsp crème fraîche
snipped chives, to serve

Takes 40–45 minutes, plus cooling
Makes 8

1 Fry the mushrooms in the butter for 3 minutes. Remove from the heat and reserve a good spoonful. Add the flour, blend with milk and return to the heat, stirring to make a thick sauce. Stir in the cheese, season and leave to cool.
2 Preheat oven to 200°C/fan 180°C/gas 6. Butter 8 x 150ml soufflé dishes and line the bases with non-stick baking paper. Stir the egg yolks into the cheese mixture. In a separate bowl, whisk the whites until stiff then folding into the soufflé mixture. Spoon into the dishes and place in a roasting tin. Fill with water to halfway up the dishes' sides. Bake for 15 minutes until golden. Leave to cool (they will sink). They can be baked up to 2 days ahead.
3 To serve, preheat the oven to 190°C/fan170°C/gas 5. Turn the soufflés out and peel off the lining paper. Put them on a baking sheet lined with squares of baking paper. Top with crème fraîche, a little cheese and the reserved mushrooms. Bake for 10–15 minutes until risen and warmed through. Sprinkle with chives and serve.

• Per soufflé 170 kcalories, protein 8g, carbohydrate 5g, fat 14g, saturated fat 8g, fibre none, sugar 2g, salt 0.41g

No wonder mussels are a bistro staple – they're cheap to buy but taste a million dollars when steamed with a little alcohol, cream and bacon.

Mussels steamed with cider and bacon

a small knob of butter
6 bacon rashers, chopped, or a 140g/5oz piece, cut into small cubes
2 shallots, finely sliced
small bunch of thyme, leaves stripped
1.5kg/3lb 5oz small mussels, scrubbed and bearded
1 glass of cider (about 150ml/¼ pint)
2 tbsp crème fraîche (optional)
crusty bread, to serve

Takes 20 minutes, plus mussels preparation • Serves 2 as a main, 4 as a starter

1 Heat the butter in a pan large enough to easily fit the mussels, then fry the bacon for 4 minutes, turning occasionally until it starts to crisp. Throw in the shallots and thyme leaves, and cook for 1 minute until softened.
2 Turn up the heat to High and add the mussels to the pan, then pour over the cider. Put a lid on the pan, give it a good shake, then cook the mussels for 5–7 minutes, shaking the pan occasionally, until all the mussels have opened. Discard any that don't open.
3 Use a slotted spoon to scoop the mussels into individual bowls and place the pan back on the heat. Bring the juices to the boil and stir in the crème fraîche, if using. Pour the sauce over the mussels. Serve with hunks of crusty bread for mopping up the sauce.

• Per serving (2, with crème fraîche) 367 kcalories, protein 39g, carbohydrate 8g, fat 18g, saturated fat 6g, fibre none, sugar 2g, salt 4.45g

This veggie main course can be put together a day ahead and left in the fridge, ready to cook at a moment's notice, or frozen well in advance.

Squash, ricotta and sage pasta bake

1 squash, about 1kg/2lb 3oz, chopped into chunks
2 tbsp olive oil
200ml crème fraîche
50g/2oz parmesan, finely grated
12 dried sheets lasagne
250g tub ricotta
a small bunch of sage leaves, half chopped and half left whole

Takes 1 hour 20 minutes • Serves 6

1 Preheat the oven to 220°C/fan 200°C/gas 7. Toss the squash with the olive oil in a roasting tin, then roast for 30 minutes until soft and golden. Meanwhile, mix the crème fraîche with half the parmesan. Boil the lasagne sheets for 5 minutes and toss in a little oil.

2 Leave the squash to cool slightly, then peel away the skin from the flesh. In a separate bowl, beat the ricotta with the chopped sage and remaining parmesan, then gently fold through the squash.

3 Assemble the bake. Spread a little of the crème fraîche mix over the bottom of a gratin dish, then lay some lasagne sheets over, then some ricotta and squash mix and more crème fraîche. Repeat saving some crème fraîche for the top. Spread the crème fraîche over the top layer of lasagne, then scatter with the sage leaves. Bake for 25 minutes until bubbling and golden.

• Per serving 445 kcalories, protein 15g, carbohydrate 40g, fat 26g, saturated fat 14g, fibre 3g, sugar 8g, salt 0.36g

The perfect dish for relaxed entertaining: bring a pan of oozing risotto to the table, break some crusty bread and tuck in.

Herb and parmesan risotto

50g/2oz butter
1 onion, finely chopped
300g/10oz risotto rice
1 small glass white wine
1.5 litres/2¾ pints hot vegetable stock
50g/2oz parmesan (half finely grated, half shaved)
2 handfuls of soft herbs (including basil and chives), half chopped and half left whole
2 tbsp olive oil
1 tbsp balsamic vinegar
crusty bread, to serve

Takes 50 minutes • Serves 4

1 Melt half the butter over a medium heat. Stir in the onion and sweat for 8–10 minutes until soft, stirring occasionally. Add the rice to the onion, and stir continuously until the edges of the grains start to look transparent.
2 Pour in the wine and simmer until totally evaporated. Add the stock, a ladleful at a time, stirring with each addition. Continue doing this for 25–30 minutes, until the rice is cooked but has a firm bite.
3 When the rice is cooked, turn off the heat, stir in the grated parmesan, the remaining butter, the chopped herbs and half the oil, then season. Roughly chop the remaining chives, then mix with the whole herb leaves, remaining olive oil and the balsamic vinegar. Serve the risotto in bowls topped with some of the herb salad and parmesan shavings.

• Per serving 496 kcalories, protein 13g, carbohydrate 67g, fat 21g, saturated fat 10g, fibre 4g, sugar 7g, salt 0.93g

No one will ever turn down a roast chicken – especially not one roasted with garlic, herbs and lemon. Delicious.

Roast chicken with lemon, garlic and rosemary

2 lemons
1 chicken, about 1.8kg/4lb
6 bay leaves
small bunch of rosemary, broken into sprigs
2 whole garlic heads, cut across the middle
1.5kg/3lb 5oz potatoes, peeled and quartered
2 tbsp sunflower oil
50g/2oz butter, very soft
green vegetables, to serve

Takes 1¾ hours • Serves 4

1 Preheat oven to 200°C/fan 180°C/gas 6. Halve a lemon and prick one half all over with a knife. Cut the rest into wedges. Put the lemon half, a bay leaf, a few sprigs of rosemary and one half head of garlic inside the chicken cavity.
2 Tip the potatoes and remaining garlic into the roasting tin, toss with the oil and season. Push the potatoes to the edges and sit the chicken in the middle. Brush the chicken all over with the butter and make sure the potatoes are evenly spaced.
3 Roast for 1 hour 20 minutes, brushing twice with more butter during cooking. Lift the bird out of the tin, cover, then leave to rest.
4 Turn the oven up to 220°C/fan 200°C/gas 7. Toss the potatoes, remaining herbs and lemon wedges in the pan juices, then roast for 15–20 minutes, turning once, until golden. Serve your roast with simple green vegetables, such as broccoli.

• Per serving 800 kcalories, protein 50g, carbohydrate 67g, fat 39g, saturated fat 13g, fibre 5g, sugar 4g, salt 1.93g

Sardines are inexpensive and widely available because their stocks are sustainable. They're packed with health-giving oils and a perfect match for this punchy summer salad.

Sardines with Sicilian fennel salad

zest and juice of 1 lemon
bunch of parsley, half the leaves finely chopped, half left whole
1 small garlic clove, finely chopped
1 fennel bulb, with fronds
50g/2oz toasted pine nuts
50g/2oz raisins
a handful of green olives, chopped
3 tbsp olive oil, plus extra for drizzling
4 large sardines, scaled and gutted
a handful of flaky sea salt

Takes 30 minutes • Serves 2
(easily doubled)

1 Mix the lemon zest, chopped parsley and garlic together, then set aside. Pick the fronds from the fennel and set aside. Halve the fennel bulb and finely slice. Make the salad by mixing the sliced fennel and fronds with the pine nuts, raisins, olives and whole parsley leaves. Dress with the olive oil and lemon juice.

2 Heat barbecue of griddle pan over a medium heat. Season the fish with the salt (this stops them sticking). Griddle or barbecue for 2–3 minutes on each side until the eyes turn white. Sprinkle the fish with the parsley mix and lift on to plates. Drizzle with oil and serve with the salad.

• Per serving 663 kcalories, protein 34g, carbohydrate 20g, fat 50g, saturated fat 7g, fibre 3g, sugar 20g, salt 1.49g

Rich, sticky, dark and packed with flavour, this is the kind of dish that puts a smile on everyone's face, even on the bleakest winter day.

Braised beef with red onions and wild mushrooms

1.5kg/3lb 5oz beef braising steak, thickly sliced
3 red onions, thinly sliced
600ml/1pint boiling water
15g/½oz dried porcini mushrooms
3 tbsp olive oil
1 tbsp plain flour
425ml/¾ pint port or red wine
250g/9oz chestnut mushrooms, whole, or halved if large
handful of chopped parsley, to serve

Takes 3½ hours • Serves 6–8

1 Preheat oven to 160°C/fan 140°C/gas 3. Pat the beef dry with kitchen paper and season both sides. Pour the boiling water over the dried mushrooms. Soak for 30 minutes then strain, reserving the juices.
2 Heat half the oil in a casserole, then add the meat in batches and fry on both sides until browned. Remove the meat from the pan, pour in the remaining oil, fry the onions for 10 minutes until softened. Return the meat to the pan, sprinkle in the flour and cook for 1 minute.
3 Add the port or wine, mushroom liquid and soaked mushrooms. Bring to the boil, season, then cover and cook for 1½–2 hours until tender. Check after 1 hour. If the sauce looks like it's getting too thick, add a splash of boiling water.
4 Taste and season, then add the chestnut mushrooms and cook for a further 10 minutes. Serve, sprinkled with chopped parsley.

• Per serving (8) 570 kcalories, protein 54g, carbohydrate 17g, fat 28g, saturated fat 10g, fibre 2g, sugar 13g, salt 0.4g

The longer you cook duck legs, the more meltingly tender they become, so it's almost impossible to overcook them. They go well with mellow Moroccan spicing and the sweet flavours of honey and fresh fruit.

Duck tagine with clementines

6 duck legs
200g/8oz shallots, peeled
2 tsp each ground coriander, cumin, ginger, and paprika
600ml/1 pint vegetable stock
2 tsp clear honey
juice of 1 lemon
6 small firm clementines, peeled
3 tbsp chopped coriander
2 tbsp toasted sesame seeds
couscous, to serve (optional)

Takes 2½ hours • Serves 6

1 Preheat oven to 190°C/fan 170°C/gas 5. Put the duck legs in one layer in a large roasting tin or in two smaller ones. Sprinkle with salt, then roast for 45 minutes. Remove the duck legs to a dish and spoon 3 tablespoons of the duck fat into a large pan (reserve the remainder of fat).
2 Add the shallots to the pan and fry briefly until just starting to colour. Sprinkle in the spices and mix well. Add the stock, honey, lemon juice, salt and pepper then bring to the boil. Sit the duck legs on top, cover tightly and cook over a gentle heat for 1–1¼ hours until the meat is tender.
3 Meanwhile, heat 1 tablespoon of the duck fat in a frying pan, add the whole clementines and fry all over until glistening and starting to brown. Add to the pan with the duck and cook for a further 15 minutes, then sprinkle with the coriander and sesame seeds. This dish goes really well with couscous.

• Per serving 437 kcalories, protein 48g, carbohydrate 9g, fat 23g, saturated fat 6g, fibre 2g, sugar 7g, salt 0.62g

This is a wonderful dish for winter. Serve with a big bowl of mashed potatoes, and a seasonal salad of bitter leaves such as chicory or curly endive, that will cut through the richness of the pork.

Slow-cooked pork and red cabbage

1.5kg/3lb 5oz pork shoulder
1 rounded tsp black peppercorns, crushed
1 tbsp thyme leaves
3 tbsp olive oil
2 onions, chopped
1kg/2lb 3oz red cabbage, finely shredded
2 apples, peeled, cored and cut into eighths
425ml/¾ pint red wine
200g pack vacuum-packed chestnuts
2 tbsp cranberry or redcurrant jelly
mashed potatoes, and green salad to serve (optional)

Takes 2 hours 40 minutes • Serves 6

1 Preheat oven to 160°C/fan 140°C/gas 3. Cut the pork into 3cm slices. Sprinkle with the crushed peppercorns, thyme and some salt.
2 Heat 2 tablespoons of the oil in a large flameproof casserole, then add the onions and fry until lightly browned. Add the cabbage, stir well, then add the apples and wine, and cook until the cabbage starts to soften. Finally, add the chestnuts, 1 tablespoon of the jelly, some seasoning, and bring to the boil. Cover and simmer for 5 minutes.
3 Meanwhile, heat the remaining oil in a frying pan, add the pork and fry on both sides until browned, then stir in the remaining jelly. Cook for a few minutes until the pork is deeply brown. Arrange over the cabbage in the casserole. Pour a little boiling water into the frying pan, stir well and scrape off any bits on the bottom of the pan, then pour over the pork.
4 Cover the casserole tightly with a lid and cook for 1¼–1½ hours until the pork is very tender.

• Per serving 770 kcalories, protein 49g, carbohydrate 33g, fat 48g, saturated fat 17g, fibre 7g, sugar 21g, salt 0.48g

Chicken with a tasty tomato sauce makes an easy Friday-night supper for friends.

Tomato and crispy crumb chicken

4 boneless skinless chicken breasts
2 thick slices wholemeal bread
2 tsp dried mixed herbs
400g can chopped tomatoes
1 garlic clove, crushed
1 tsp balsamic vinegar (optional)
2 tsp tomato purée
350g/12oz green beans

Takes 40 minutes • Serves 4

1 Preheat the oven to 190°C/fan 170°C/gas 5. Split the chicken breasts almost in half and open them out like a book. Put them in a non-stick roasting tin.
2 Whiz the bread in a food processor to make breadcrumbs and mix with the herbs. Drain the tomatoes and mix with the garlic, vinegar (if using) and tomato purée. Spread the sauce over the chicken and sprinkle with the breadcrumbs. Bake for 20–25 minutes until the chicken is tender.
3 Meanwhile, steam the beans for 5–7 minutes until just tender. Serve the chicken on a bed of beans.

• Per serving 238 kcalories, protein 39g, carbohydrate 16g, fat 3g, saturated fat 1g, fibre none, sugar 5g, salt 0.66g

This classic combination of flavours works really well in a tortilla – a thick omelette that's quick to make and a brilliant way to use up leftover potatoes and cheese.

Cheese, leek and potato tortilla

a knob of butter, for frying
1 leek, thinly sliced
225g/8oz cooked and cooled potatoes
6 eggs
85g/3oz cheddar
1 tbsp finely chopped sage, or 1 tsp dried sage (optional)
green salad, to serve

Takes 15 minutes • Serves 4

1 Melt a knob of butter in a medium, non-stick frying pan, then gently cook the leek for 5 minutes until softened. Meanwhile, cut the potatoes in half, then into slices about ½cm thick. Beat the eggs, season, then stir in the cheese and the sage (if using).
2 Add a little extra butter to the pan if needed, tip in the potatoes, then the egg mixture. Gently stir the potato and leek together, then turn the heat to low and cook for 10 minutes until nearly set. Put under a hot grill to cook for a couple of minutes more until the top is set and golden. Slice into wedges and serve with a green salad.

• Per serving 277 kcalories, protein 16g, carbohydrate 11g, fat 19g, saturated fat 9g, fibre 1g, sugar 1g, salt 0.81g

Leftover chicken goes a long way in this hearty pie.

Lemon and mushroom chicken pie

a knob of butter, for frying
1 onion, finely chopped
100g/4oz mushrooms, sliced
zest of 1 lemon
300g/10oz cooked leftover chicken, torn into strips
3 tbsp crème fraîche
½ × 375g pack ready-rolled puff pastry
mash and green veg, to serve (optional)

Takes 30 minutes • Serves 2–3

1 Preheat oven to 200°C/fan 180°C/gas 6. Melt a knob of butter in a frying pan, tip in the onion, then gently fry for a couple of minutes until soft. Stir in the mushrooms, then cook for 3 minutes more until lightly browned. Stir through the lemon zest and chicken. Place in a small pie dish, then dollop over 2½ tablespoons of the crème fraîche.
2 Lay the pastry over the dish and pinch around the edges to seal well. Cut away the excess pastry, then make a small slit in the centre of the pie. Brush the remaining crème fraîche all over the pastry, then bake for 25 minutes until the pastry is risen, crisp, and golden. Serve the pie on its own or with mash and green veg.

• Per serving (3) 721 kcalories, protein 53g, carbohydrate 40g, fat 40g, saturated fat 18g, fibre 1g, sugar 5g, salt 1.05g

It's amazing what you can throw together with a pack of pastry and a bit of imagination. We've used peppers, artichokes and mozzarella, but you can use ham, any cheese, anchovies or olives.

Fridge or freezer tarts

375g pack ready-rolled puff pastry
4 tbsp green pesto or other pasta sauce
140g/5oz frozen sliced roasted peppers
140g/5oz artichokes, from a jar or frozen (about 3 wedges per serving)
125g ball mozzarella, torn or 85g/3oz hard cheese, grated
green salad, to serve

Takes about 30 minutes • Serves 4

1 Preheat oven to 200°C/fan 180°C/gas 6. Unroll the pastry and cut into 4 rectangles. Take a sharp knife and lightly score a 1cm edge inside each rectangle, taking care that you don't cut all the way through the pastry. Put on a baking sheet.

2 Spread 1 tablespoon of pesto or pasta sauce onto each pastry slice, staying inside the border, then pile up the peppers and artichokes on top. Bake in the oven for 15 minutes until the pastry is starting to brown.

3 Scatter the cheese over the veg. Return to the oven for 5–7 minutes until the pastry is crisp and the cheese has melted. Serve with a green salad.

• Per serving 515 kcalories, protein 16g, carbohydrate 42g, fat 33g, saturated fat 14g, fibre 3g, sugar 6g, salt 1.98g

Pre-packed sandwiches can be expensive and disappointing, so why not take your own classic club to work instead. You can grill the bacon the night before, then assemble and eat the next day.

Turkey and bacon club

2 rashers streaky bacon
butter, for spreading
3 slices bread (white or brown, or a mix)
1 thick slice cooked turkey
a little mayonnaise and mustard
a few lettuce leaves, shredded
½ avocado, sliced

Takes 10 minutes • Serves 1

1 Grill the bacon until crisp, then drain on kitchen paper (do this the night before, if you like).
2 Butter one slice of bread on one side, then cover with the turkey, a little mayonnaise and the lettuce. Butter both sides of the next slice of bread, and put on top of the turkey. Spread a little mustard over the bread, then arrange the bacon on top with the sliced avocado. Butter the last slice of bread on one side and put on top, buttered side down.
3 Press the sandwich down lightly, then cut in half on the diagonal.

• Per serving 745 kcalories, protein 31g, carbohydrate 54g, fat 46g, saturated fat 19g, fibre 4g, sugar 4g, salt 3.44g

Mediterranean flavours come together beautifully in this colourful salad that's ideal for lunchboxes. Make it in summer when the veg are at their best, and cheapest.

Aubergine couscous salad

1 large aubergine, sliced into
1cm rounds
3 tbsp olive oil
140g/5oz couscous
225ml/8fl oz hot vegetable stock
200g/8oz cherry tomatoes, halved
a handful of mint leaves, roughly
chopped
100g log firm goat's cheese, cubed
juice of ½ lemon

Takes 15 minutes • Serves 2
(easily doubled)

1 Heat grill to High. Put the aubergine on a baking sheet, brush with a little of the oil and season. Grill for about 15 minutes until browned and softened, turning and brushing with more oil halfway through.
2 Meanwhile, tip the couscous into a large bowl, pour over the stock, then cover and leave for 10 minutes.
3 Mix together the tomatoes, mint, goat's cheese and remaining oil. Fluff up the couscous with a fork, then stir in the aubergine, tomato mixture and lemon juice and serve.

• Per serving 523 kcalories, protein 18g, carbohydrate 45g, fat 31g, saturated fat 11g, fibre 6g, sugar 9g, salt 1.08g

Kids love these tasty little biscuits – pack some up with a few slices of ham, carrot sticks and cherry tomatoes for a healthy snack and happy faces.

Cheese stackers

100g/4oz olive oil spread
50g/2oz Emmenthal or cheddar cheese, finely grated
85g/3oz mozzarella cheese, grated
200g/8oz malted grain flour
1 tsp baking powder
pinch of English mustard powder (optional)
1 tbsp mixed seeds

Takes 30 minutes • Makes about 30

1 Preheat oven to 190°C/fan 170°C/gas 5. Line two baking sheets with non-stick baking parchment. Put the olive oil spread into a bowl and mix in the cheeses. Add the flour, baking powder, mustard powder, if using, a pinch of salt and the mixed seeds, then stir to combine. Squeeze the mixture together with your hands. Roll the mixture into balls the size of cherry tomatoes. Space out on the baking sheet, then flatten each one with the palm of your hand (or roll out the dough and use a cookie cutter to make fun shapes).
2 Prick each biscuit several times with a fork, then bake for 12–15 minutes until golden. Cool, then store in an airtight container for up to a week.

• Per stacker 70 kcalories, protein 2g, carbohydrate 5g, fat 5g, saturated fat 1g, fibre 1g, sugar none, salt 0.10g

If you like duck and hoisin sauce but worry about the high fat content, try these easy wraps instead. With no lettuce to turn soggy, they make great food to go and are equally good using turkey too.

Chicken hoisin wraps

2 tortilla wraps
4 tsp hoisin sauce
100g/4oz cooked chicken, shredded
¼ cucumber, cut into sticks
4 spring onions, shredded

Takes 5 minutes • Serves 2

1 Warm the tortillas in the microwave or in a dry frying pan.
2 Thinly spread each tortilla with 2 teaspoons of the hoisin sauce. Scatter with the chicken, cucumber and shredded spring onion, then wrap and eat.

• Per serving 182 kcalories, protein 18.6g, carbohydrate 20.1g, fat 3.6g, saturated fat 0.9g, fibre 1.4g, sugar 4.7g, salt 0.85g

There's a chance you'll already have most of the ingredients for this low-fat salad in your storecupboard and fridge.

Honey-mustard chicken pasta

300g/10oz farfalle or other pasta shape
3 tbsp reduced-fat mayonnaise (use full-fat, if you prefer)
1 heaped tsp wholegrain mustard
1 tsp clear honey
300g/10oz cooked chicken, torn into rough pieces
4 spring onions, thinly sliced (or use ½ red onion, thinly sliced)
a small bunch of basil, leaves roughly torn
4 tomatoes, quartered then halved

Takes 20 minutes • Serves 4 (easily halved)

1 Cook the pasta according to the packet instructions, drain and cool under running water.

2 Mix the mayonnaise with the mustard and honey in a large bowl and loosen with a little water to make a dressing the consistency of double cream. Add the pasta, chicken, spring onions or red onion, basil and tomatoes, season to taste, then gently mix together to serve.

• Per serving 450 kcalories, protein 31g, carbohydrate 62g, fat 11g, saturated fat 3g, fibre 3g, sugar 6g, salt 0.55g

You can't go wrong with a good basic quiche. Wrap up slices for a tasty take-away lunch, or serve at home with a fresh green salad.

Sticky onion and cheddar quiche

5 small onions (500g/1lb 2oz in total), halved and finely sliced
25g/1oz butter
2 eggs
284ml pot double cream
140g/5oz mature cheddar, coarsely grated

FOR THE PASTRY
300g/10oz plain flour, plus extra for dusting
140g/5oz cold butter, cut into pieces

Takes 1 hour 20 minutes • Serves 8

1 First make the pastry. Tip the flour and butter into a processor, then whiz until it forms crumbs. Add 8 tablespoons of cold water, then pulse to a dough. Roll into a ball and chill for 10 minutes. Roll out the pastry on a floured surface and use to line a 25cm tart tin, with a little overhang. Chill for 20 minutes.
2 Meanwhile, over a medium heat, soften the onions in the butter for 20 minutes, until golden. Preheat oven to 200°C/fan 180°C/gas 6.
3 Line the pastry with a large circle of greaseproof paper, then fill with baking beans. Blind-bake for 20 minutes. Remove the paper and beans then cook for 10 minutes until brown.
4 Beat together the eggs and cream, then stir in the onions and half the cheese, and season. Pour the mixture into the case, top with the remaining cheese, then bake for 20–25 minutes until set and golden. Cool, then trim the edges of the pastry, turn out of the tin and serve in slices.

• Per serving 567 kcalories, protein 11g, carbohydrate 33g, fat 44g, saturated fat 26g, fibre 2g, sugar 5g, salt 0.72g

Don't chuck out stale bread – this salad has to be made with bread that's past its best. You can use ciabatta or any country loaf with a good crust and even pitta bread.

Tuna and caper panzanella

3 slices ciabatta (preferably a day or two old)
4–5 tomatoes
½ cucumber
handful of basil leaves
200g can tuna in brine
2 tsp capers, drained and roughly chopped
2 tbsp wine vinegar, any type
4 tbsp olive oil

Takes 15 minutes • Serves 2

1 Dip the bread very briefly into cold water, then squeeze it well and crumble it into a bowl. Halve the tomatoes and squeeze out the seeds, then roughly chop the flesh. Chop the cucumber into small chunks.
2 Add the tomato and cucumber to the bread, then tear in the basil leaves. Drain and flake the tuna into chunks, then add to the bread with the capers, vinegar, oil and salt and pepper to taste. Mix everything together well and serve.

• Per serving 463 kcalories, protein 27g, carbohydrate 21g, fat 31g, saturated fat 5g, fibre 3g, sugar 6g, salt 1.35g

Take what's left of the fruit bowl and some leftover ham or turkey, and you've got a great family salad in 15 minutes flat. If you're taking the salad to work, keep the dressing separate until you want to eat.

Turkey and ham salad

180g bag Continental salad
2 ripe pears or crisp apples
a good handful of chopped walnuts
(or use hazelnuts or pine nuts)
3 slices each turkey and ham

FOR THE DRESSING
1 small red onion, finely chopped
1 tbsp wine vinegar, any type
2 tsp clear honey
125g pot low-fat natural yogurt

Takes 15 minutes • Serves 4
(easily halved)

1 Tip the bag of salad on to a large platter. Quarter, core and slice the pears or apples, then scatter over the salad leaves with the walnuts.
2 Cut the turkey and ham into strips and scatter over the top.
3 Mix together all the dressing ingredients in a small bowl, then drizzle over the salad just before serving.

• Per serving 240 kcalories, protein 27g, carbohydrate 14g, fat 9g, saturated fat 2g, fibre 3g, sugar 14g, salt 1.67g

This easy-to-make rice, with its handy measurements, is perfect for older kids to fix for themselves.

Raid-the-fridge rice

6 rashers streaky or back bacon, chopped
a handful of mushrooms, halved
1 small onion, chopped
1 tbsp sunflower oil
1 garlic clove, crushed
150g/5½oz (½ a mug) long grain rice
300ml/½pint (1 mug) hot chicken or vegetable stock
a handful of cheddar or other hard cheese, grated

Takes 35 minutes • Serves 2

1 Heat a large non-stick pan and tip in the bacon. Fry for a few minutes over a medium heat until the fat starts to run out. Add the mushrooms, turn up the heat a little, then fry for another 3–4 minutes until the mushrooms are golden and the bacon is crisp. Tip on to a heatproof plate and keep warm.

2 Using the same pan, soften the onion in the oil for 5 minutes. Add the garlic, fry for 1 minute, then tip in the rice and stock, and bring to the boil. Turn the heat down to a gentle simmer for 10 minutes until almost all of the liquid has gone. Take off the heat, stir, then cover for 5 minutes to finish cooking in its own steam.

3 Stir most of the cheese through the rice, then season. Serve in bowls topped with the bacon and mushrooms and the rest of the cheese sprinkled over.

• Per serving 549 kcalories, protein 19g, carbohydrate 68g, fat 24g, saturated fat 9g, fibre 1g, sugar 2g, salt 2.32g

A ripe avocado makes a fab lunch instead of the usual salad or sandwiches. Rub the cut and stoned avocado with a little lemon juice if you're not planning to tuck in straight away.

Houmous avocado with tomato salad

1 small red onion, sliced
2 tomatoes, chopped
a handful of pitted olives
a squeeze of lemon juice
olive oil, for drizzling
1 avocado
2 tbsp houmous
toasted bread, to serve

Takes 5 minutes • Serves 2

1 Combine the onion, tomatoes and olives with the lemon juice. Drizzle with oil and season to taste.
2 Halve and stone the avocado, then spoon the houmous into the space where the stone was. Scatter with the tomato salad, drizzle with a little more oil, then serve with toasted bread.

• Per serving 436 kcalories, protein 4.6g, carbohydrate 8.8g, fat 42.7g, saturated fat 5.4g, fibre 7g, sugar 5.3g, salt 0.46g

Make different versions of this salad by replacing the ham with flaked smoked mackerel, peeled prawns, salami or chopped cheese.

Ham and beetroot salad bowl

100g/4oz frozen peas
175g/6oz cooked beetroot
(not in vinegar)
2 spring onions, thinly sliced
2 tbsp Greek yogurt
2 tsp horseradish sauce
½ iceberg lettuce, shredded
100g/4oz thin sliced ham

Takes 15 minutes • Serves 2

1 Pour boiling water over the peas and leave for 2 minutes, then drain well. Chop the beetroot into cubes.
2 Tip the peas, beetroot and spring onions into a bowl, and mix well. In another bowl, combine the yogurt and horseradish, then add about 1 tablespoon of boiling water to make a pouring dressing.
3 Pile the lettuce into two bowls, then spoon over the beetroot mix in each. Thinly drizzle the dressing over the salad and top with ham.

• Per serving 166 kcalories, protein 16g, carbohydrate 17g, fat 4g, saturated fat 2g, fibre 5g, sugar 13g, salt 1.92g

Versatile and tasty, this spread is brilliant stuffed into pitta with carrots, celery and cucumber sticks, or used as you would houmous.

Best bean spread

410g can butter beans, drained
2 tbsp olive oil
2 tbsp lemon juice
125g light garlic and herb cheese (we used Boursin Light)

Takes 10 minutes • Serves 4

1 Put the butter beans into a food processor, then pour in the olive oil and lemon juice. Add a pinch of salt and some freshly ground black pepper. Whizz together to make a smooth paste.
2 Add the garlic and herb cheese, blend until smooth, then put into a sealable container and chill. Will keep for up to 3 days.

• Per serving 151 kcalories, protein 5.7g, carbohydrate 8.8g, fat 10.6g, saturated fat 3.8g, fibre 2.8g, sugar 1.8g, salt 0.97g

A simple, low-fat midweek dish using leftover rice, that's perfect for those days when you are pushed for time but need to feed the family.

Spicy chicken rice

200g pack spicy cooked chicken fillets
250g/9oz leftover cooked rice or 250g pouch pre-cooked rice
⅓ cucumber, finely chopped
2 carrots, coarsely grated
20g pack mint leaves, roughly chopped
150g low-fat natural yogurt
1 tsp clear honey
a pinch of chilli powder

Takes 15 minutes • Serves 2

1 Chop the chicken into bite-sized pieces and mix with the rice, cucumber and carrots.
2 Mix half the mint with the yogurt, honey, chilli powder and seasoning. Stir into the rice and sprinkle with the remaining mint.

• Per serving 357 kcalories, protein 31g, carbohydrate 57g, fat 2g, saturated fat 1g, fibre 3g, sugar 19g, salt 0.99g

Sweet potatoes cook down to make a silky soup that tastes luxurious but costs very little.

Speedy sweet potato soup with coconut

1 tbsp vegetable oil
1 onion, chopped
1–2 tsp Thai curry paste
(red or green)
750g/1lb 10oz sweet potatoes,
peeled and grated
1 litre/1¾ pints hot vegetable stock
½ sachet creamed coconut (or use
¼ can reduced-fat coconut milk)
a handful of coriander leaves,
roughly chopped, to garnish
mini naan breads, to serve

Takes 20 minutes • Serves 4

1 Heat the oil in a deep pan, then add the onion and soften it over a low heat for 4–5 minutes. Stir in the curry paste and cook for 1 minute more until fragrant. Add the grated sweet potatoes and stock, then bring quickly to the boil, simmering for 5 minutes until the potatoes are tender.
2 Remove the soup from the heat, stir in the coconut and some seasoning, then blend until smooth. Sprinkle with coriander and serve with warm mini naan breads.

• Per serving 240 kcalories, protein 4g, carbohydrate 45g, fat 6g, saturated fat 3g, fibre 6g, sugar 15g, salt 0.56g

This simple soup will become a favourite standby for a quick spring lunch. In any other season, use frozen mixed green veg instead of fresh.

Springtime minestrone

200g/8oz mixed green vegetables (we used asparagus, broad beans and spring onions)
700ml/1¼ pints hot vegetable stock
140g/5oz cooked pasta (spaghetti chopped into small pieces works well)
215g can butter beans, rinsed and drained
3 tbsp green pesto

Takes 10 minutes • Serves 4

1 Place the green vegetables in a medium-sized pan, then pour over the stock. Bring to the boil, then reduce the heat and simmer until the vegetables are cooked through, about 3 minutes.
2 Stir in the cooked pasta, beans and 1 tablespoon of the pesto. Warm through, then ladle into bowls and top each with another drizzle of pesto.

• Per serving 125 kcalories, protein 8g, carbohydrate 16g, fat 4g, saturated fat 1g, fibre 4g, sugar 3g, salt 0.7g

Everyone loves this soup and it's simplicity itself to make a batch using just a few low-cost ingredients.

Carrot and coriander soup

1 tbsp vegetable oil
1 onion, chopped
1 tsp ground coriander
1 potato, peeled and chopped
450g/1lb carrots, peeled and chopped
1.2 litres/2 pints hot vegetable or chicken stock
a handful of coriander (about ½ a supermarket pack)

Takes 40 minutes • Serves 4

1 Heat the oil in a large pan, add the onion, then fry for 5 minutes until softened. Stir in the ground coriander and potato, then cook for 1 minute. Add the carrots and stock, bring to the boil, then lower the heat. Cover and cook for 20 minutes until the carrots are tender.

2 Tip into a food processor with most of the coriander and blitz until smooth (you may need to do this in two batches). Return the soup to the pan, taste, add salt if necessary, then reheat to serve. Garnish with the remaining coriander leaves.

• Per serving 115 kcalories, protein 3g, carbohydrate 19g, fat 4g, saturated fat 1g, fibre 5g, sugar 12g, salt 0.46g

Although creamy in both name and texture, this soup actually has no cream added. The generous chunks of chicken and vegetables make it a real meal in a bowl.

Creamy chicken soup

85g/3oz butter
1 small onion, roughly chopped
1 large carrot, cut into small chunks
300g/10oz floury potatoes, cut into
small chunks
1 large leek, trimmed and
thinly sliced
1 heaped tbsp fresh thyme leaves,
or 1 tsp dried
50g/2oz plain flour
1.3 litres/2¼ pints hot chicken stock
200g/8oz cooked chicken, torn into
big chunks
crusty bread, to serve

Takes 40 minutes • Serves 4

1 Melt 25g of the butter in a large, wide pan and heat until bubbling. Add the onion and fry for 3–4 minutes until just starting to colour. Stir in the carrot and potatoes, and fry for 4 minutes, then add the leek and thyme, and cook for 3 more minutes. Set aside.
2 Melt the remaining butter in a medium pan. When bubbling, stir in the flour and keep stirring for 3–4 minutes until pale golden. With the pan still on the heat, gradually pour in the hot stock, stirring constantly as you go. When all the stock has been added, pour it into the pan of vegetables, simmer, then cook gently for 8–10 minutes, giving it all an occasional stir.
3 Stir in the chicken and seasoning. Warm through, and serve with crusty bread.

• Per serving 449 kcalories, protein 28g, carbohydrate 32g, fat 24g, saturated fat 13g, fibre 4g, sugar 8g, salt 1.10g

Keep smoked haddock fillets and sweetcorn in the freezer, and add a few storecupboard staples for this tasty chowder.

Sweetcorn and haddock chowder

a knob of butter
2 rashers streaky bacon, chopped
1 onion, finely chopped
500ml/18fl oz milk
350g/12oz potatoes (about
2 medium), cut into small cubes
300g/10oz frozen smoked haddock
fillets (about 2)
140g/5oz frozen sweetcorn
chopped parsley, to garnish
(optional)
crusty bread, to serve

Takes 30 minutes • Serves 2

1 Heat the butter in a large pan. Tip in the bacon, then cook until starting to brown. Add the onion, cook until soft, then pour over the milk and stir through the potatoes. Bring to the boil, then simmer for 5 minutes.
2 Add the haddock, then leave to cook gently for another 10 minutes. By now the fish should have defrosted so you can break it up into large chunks. Stir through the sweetcorn, then cook for another few minutes until the fish is cooked through and the sweetcorn has defrosted. Scatter over the parsley, if using. Serve with plenty of crusty bread.

• Per serving 550 kcalories, protein 47g, carbohydrate 59g, fat 16g, saturated fat 7g, fibre 4g, sugar 18g, salt 3.92g

Although French in origin, onion soup feels very British too, and we've added cider and cheddar to this one to make it even more so.

British onion soup

50g/2oz butter or 2 tbsp dripping
1kg/2lb 3oz onions, finely sliced
1 tbsp golden caster sugar
a few sprigs of thyme
3 bay leaves
150ml/¼ pint cider
1 litre/1¾ pints hot vegetable
or chicken stock

FOR THE TOP
4 thick slices from a round
country loaf
100g/4oz mature cheddar, grated
a large handful of parsley, chopped

Takes 1¾ hours • Serves 4

1 Heat most of the butter or dripping in a pan, then add the onions, sugar and herbs. Season and cook, uncovered, over a low heat, stirring occasionally, for up to 40 minutes until sticky and brown. Pour in the cider and simmer until reduced by half. Pour in the stock, bring to the boil, then cook for 20 minutes.

2 To serve, heat the grill to High. Spread the bread on both sides with the remaining butter or dripping, then toast under the grill until golden. Scatter with the cheese and put back under the grill until melted. Serve the soup in bowls with a slice of the toast floating in it, scattered generously with parsley.

• Per serving 451 kcalories, protein 15g, carbohydrate 51g, fat 21g, saturated fat 12g, fibre 6g, sugar 22g, salt 1.75g

This leftover classic makes a great side dish at Christmas or any time of the year, and a delicious vegetarian main in its own right.

Spiced parsnip bubble and squeak cake

800g/1lb 12oz parsnips, chopped into chunks
1 tsp turmeric
½ Savoy cabbage or 300g/10oz Brussels sprouts, finely shredded
a large handful of frozen peas
juice of ½ lemon
50g/2oz butter
1 tsp cumin seeds
1 tbsp garam masala
a bunch of fresh coriander, chopped
1 red chilli, seeded and chopped
sprigs of fresh coriander, to serve

Takes 45 minutes • Serves 4 as a main or 8 as a side dish

1 Tip the parsnips and turmeric into a pan of cold water. Bring to the boil for 12 minutes or until they're on the brink of collapsing. Blanch the cabbage or sprouts in another pan of boiling water for 3 minutes until tender. Add the peas for the final minute, then drain well.

2 Drain the parsnips, then tip back into the pan and roughly mash with the lemon juice and half the butter. Beat in all the other ingredients except the remaining butter and coriander sprigs then season.

3 Heat the remaining butter in a large non-stick frying pan and press the parsnip mixture down into it. Cook until crisp underneath, then turn with a fish slice. (Don't worry if it breaks at this point, it will hold eventually.) Keep cooking until crisp on the other side, then slide on to a plate and flip back into the pan. Keep on doing this until you have a crisp cake. Serve cut into wedges and garnished with coriander leaves.

• Per serving 277 kcalories, protein 7g, carbohydrate 33g, fat 14g, saturated fat 7g, fibre 12g, sugar 15g, salt 0.27g

This fragrant noodle soup is just the thing when you crave something light and healthy.

Chicken noodle soup

1.3 litres/2¼ pints chicken stock
2 star anise
3cm piece fresh root ginger, sliced (no need to peel)
2 garlic cloves in skins, bruised
2 bok choi, shredded
85g/3oz medium egg noodles
4 spring onions, finely sliced
100g/4oz cooked chicken, torn into very thin shreds
a splash of soy sauce
a handful of basil leaves
1 mild plump red chilli, seeded and finely sliced
sesame oil, to serve (optional)

Takes 30 minutes • Serves 4

1 Pour the stock into a medium pan. Add the star anise, ginger and garlic, and gently simmer, without boiling, for 10 minutes. For the last 2 minutes, put the bok choi into a colander or sieve, suspend it over the pan and cover to steam the greens.
2 Drop the egg noodles into the stock, stirring to separate, then simmer for 4 minutes until tender. Throw in the spring onions and chicken. Season to taste with a splash of soy sauce. Ladle into bowls and scatter over the bok choi, basil leaves and chilli. Shake over a few drops of sesame oil, if you like.

• Per serving 132 kcalories, protein 19g, carbohydrate 5g, fat 4g, saturated fat 1g, fibre 1g, sugar 3g, salt 1.08g

With this homemade soup in the freezer, you're never short of a starter, a casual lunch, or even a late-night supper.

Leek, bacon and potato soup

25g/1oz butter
3 rashers streaky bacon, chopped, plus 4 rashers crisp streaky bacon, to serve
1 onion, chopped
400g pack trimmed leeks, sliced and well washed
3 medium potatoes, peeled and diced
1.4 litres/2½ pints hot vegetable stock
142ml pot single cream (or use milk)
toasted or warm crusty bread, to serve

Takes 40 minutes • Serves 4–6

1 Melt the butter in a large pan, then fry the bacon and onion, stirring until they start to turn golden. Tip in the leeks and potatoes, stir well, then cover and turn down the heat. Cook gently for 5 minutes, shaking the pan every now and then to make sure the mixture doesn't catch.

2 Pour in the stock, season well then bring to the boil. Cover and simmer for 20 minutes until the vegetables are soft. Leave to cool for a few minutes, then blend in a food processor in batches until smooth. Return to the pan, pour in the cream or milk and stir well. Taste and season if necessary. Serve scattered with tasty crisp bacon and toasted or warm crusty bread on the side.

• Per serving (6) 175 kcalories, protein 6g, carbohydrate 15g, fat 11g, saturated fat 6g, fibre 4g, sugar 5g, salt 0.68g

At Sunday lunch, serve up something other than roast potatoes with these tasty, cheesy chunks of swede.

Roasted swede with parmesan

1 large swede (approx 750g/1lb 10oz), peeled and cut into chips
1 tbsp olive oil, plus extra for greasing
50g/2oz parmesan, grated
1 tbsp fresh rosemary leaves, chopped
a knob of butter
2 garlic cloves, peeled

Takes 45 minutes • Serves 4

1 Preheat oven to 220°C/fan 200°C/gas 7. Tip the swede, olive oil, 40g of the parmesan and the rosemary leaves into a shallow roasting tin. Season and toss well, arranging in one layer. Sprinkle over the remaining parmesan, dot with butter, then add the garlic cloves.
2 Roast for 30–35 minutes until crisp and golden, turning halfway through cooking.

• Per serving 155 kcalories, protein 6g, carbohydrate 10g, fat 10g, saturated fat 4g, fibre 4g, sugar 9g, salt 0.34g

Braising in a little wine turns the humble leek into a soft and melting side dish. Get this in the oven and forget about it while it cooks.

Leeks braised with thyme

2 garlic cloves, finely sliced
1 tbsp chopped thyme leaves
2 tbsp butter
6 large leeks, cut into finger-thick rounds
150ml/¼ pint white wine (or more vegetable stock)
150ml/¼ pint hot vegetable stock

Takes 1 hour • Serves 4

1 Preheat oven to 180°C/fan 160°C/gas 4. Fry the garlic and thyme in the butter until soft. Add the leeks and toss in the buttery mix. Tip into a roasting tin, arranging the leeks so they lie flat in one layer. Pour over the wine and stock, loosely cover with a damp, scrunched piece of greaseproof paper, then cook in the oven for 30 minutes.
2 Remove the greaseproof paper, then return to the oven for 10 minutes until the leeks are browned. Pour over some of the buttery sauce to serve.

• Per serving 130 kcalories, protein 4g, carbohydrate 8g, fat 8g, saturated fat 5g, fibre 4g, sugar 6g, salt 0.20g

Silky-smooth pumpkin soup is a doddle to make. Try topping it with your own croutons – a thrifty way to use up stale bread.

Pumpkin soup

4 tbsp olive oil
2 onions, finely chopped
1kg/2lb 3oz pumpkin or squash,
peeled, seeded and chopped
into chunks
700ml/1¼ pints vegetable
or chicken stock
142ml pot double cream
4 slices wholemeal seeded bread,
crusts removed
a handful of pumpkin seeds

Takes 45 minutes • Serves 6

1 Heat half the oil in a large pan, then gently cook the onions for 5 minutes until soft. Add the pumpkin or squash to the pan and cook for 8–10 minutes more, stirring occasionally until it starts to soften and turn golden.
2 Pour the stock into the pan and season. Bring to the boil, then simmer for 10 minutes until the squash is very soft. Pour the cream into the pan, bring back to the boil, then whizz with an electric hand blender.
3 While the soup is cooking, cut the bread into small croutons. Heat the remaining oil in a frying pan and fry the bread until crisp. Add the pumpkin seeds to the pan, then cook for a few minutes more until toasty. Reheat the soup if necessary, taste for seasoning, then serve with croutons and seeds and drizzled with more oil, if you like.

• Per serving 317 kcalories, protein 6g, carbohydrate 20g, fat 24g, saturated fat 9g, fibre none, sugar 6g, salt 0.54g

These spicy breadcrumbs are also delicious sprinkled over other vegetables, such as cauliflower or leeks.

Broccoli with garlic and chilli breadcrumbs

500g/1lb 2oz broccoli
2 tbsp olive oil
a knob of butter
2 small garlic cloves, finely chopped
1 small red chilli, seeded and finely chopped
50g/2oz white breadcrumbs

Takes 20 minutes • Serves 4

1 Steam the broccoli for 5 minutes until tender.
2 Meanwhile, heat the oil and butter in a pan, then fry the garlic and chilli for 1 minute. Add the breadcrumbs, then fry for 5 minutes until crisp.
3 Season the broccoli, arrange in a dish, then scatter over the spicy breadcrumbs and serve immediately.

• Per serving 142 kcalories, protein 6g, carbohydrate 13g, fat 8g, saturated fat 2g, fibre 4g, sugar 3g, salt 0.31g

Roasting brings out the best in root veg. This full-flavoured mash goes particularly well with roast chicken, chorizo and blue cheese.

Roast sweet potato, squash and garlic mash

1kg/2lb 3oz butternut squash, peeled and cut into chunks
1kg/2lb 3oz sweet potatoes, peeled and cut into chunks
2 garlic bulbs
1 red chilli
3 tbsp olive oil, plus extra for drizzling

Takes 1 hour • Serves 4

1 Preheat oven to 200°C/fan 180°C/gas 6. Divide the squash and potatoes between 2 roasting tins. Halve the garlic bulbs and put them and the whole chilli into one of the tins. Toss with the olive oil and roast for 45 minutes.

2 Once the squash and potatoes are soft and golden, halve and seed the roasted chilli, then chop, discarding the seeds. Squeeze out the garlic from the cut cloves and mash everything together. Season and drizzle with a little more oil to serve.

• Per serving 434 kcalories, protein 6.8g, carbohydrate 76.1g, fat 13.6g, saturated fat 2.1g, fibre 10.5g, sugar 25.8g, salt 0.28g

Bring some new flavours and textures to good old mashed potato.
This variation just loves to be served with gammon or fish.

Mustard champ

1kg/2lb 3oz floury potatoes, peeled
and chopped
2 bunches of spring onions, sliced
50g/2oz butter
200ml/8fl oz milk
1–2 tbsp wholegrain mustard

Takes 30 minutes • Serves 4

1 Boil the potatoes in salted water for
15 minutes or until tender.
2 Meanwhile, fry the onions in half the butter
for 2 minutes until soft but still a perky green.
3 Drain the potatoes, then mash. Heat the
milk and the rest of the butter in a corner of
the pan, then beat into the mash along with
the mustard. Stir in the onions and serve.

• Per serving 320 kcalories, protein 8.3g, carbohydrate
47.1g, fat 12.3g, saturated fat 7.1g, fibre 4.2g, sugar
5.5g, salt 0.45g

Polish food is becoming increasingly popular in British supermarkets, so why not experiment with some new ingredients in this filling family soup.

Hearty sausage soup

2 large onions, sliced
2 tbsp olive oil
2 garlic cloves, thinly sliced
200g/8oz Kabanos Polish sausages, chopped
1 tsp paprika, sweet or smoked
85g/3oz brown basmati rice
1 tbsp chopped fresh thyme
2 litres/3½ pints beef stock
3 carrots, thickly sliced
100g/4oz shredded kale or cabbage
crusty bread, to serve

Takes 40 minutes • Serves 4

1 Fry the onions in the oil for 5 minutes. Add the garlic and sausage, fry for a few minutes more, then stir in the paprika, rice and thyme.
2 Pour in the stock, bring to the boil, add the carrots and some salt and pepper, cover, then simmer for 20 minutes. Stir in the kale or cabbage, and cook for 10 minutes more. Serve with crusty bread.

• Per serving 433 kcalories, protein 21g, carbohydrate 34g, fat 24g, saturated fat 6g, fibre 5g, sugar 12g, salt 3.83g

Add a little crunch to your plate with our fresh twist on coleslaw.
If you like, you can replace the fennel and shallots with a finely sliced
Spanish onion.

Red cabbage and fennel coleslaw

½ small red cabbage, shredded
2 medium carrots, coarsely grated
1 fennel bulb, cut into quarters and
shredded
2 shallots, thinly sliced
50g/2oz mayonnaise

Takes 15 minutes • Serves 4

1 Put all the vegetables in a bowl and toss well. Stir in the mayonnaise to coat the salad, then season with lots of black pepper and a little salt, and serve. Any leftovers can be stored in a sealed container in the fridge for up to 2 days.

• Per serving 117 kcalories, protein 1g, carbohydrate 6g, fat 10g, saturated fat 2g, fibre 3g, sugar 6g, salt 0.19g

When you've got rich tinned tomatoes and intense, fruity sundried tomatoes, there's no reason not to enjoy a home-made tomato soup in the depths of winter.

Rich tomato soup with pesto

a knob of butter or 1 tbsp olive oil
2 garlic cloves, crushed
5 soft sun-dried tomatoes in oil, roughly chopped
3 × 400g cans plum tomatoes
500ml/18fl oz chicken or vegetable stock
1 tsp sugar (any type), or to taste
142g pot soured cream
basil pesto, to serve
basil leaves, to garnish (optional)

Take 25 minutes • Serves 4

1 Heat the butter or oil in a large pan, then add the garlic and soften for a few minutes over a low heat. Add the sun-dried or SunBlush tomatoes, canned tomatoes, stock, sugar, and seasoning, then bring to a simmer. Let the soup bubble for 10 minutes until the tomatoes have broken down a little.
2 Whiz with a stick blender, adding half the soured cream as you do so. Taste and adjust the seasoning – add more sugar if you need to. Serve in bowls with 1 tablespoon or so of the pesto swirled on top and a little more soured cream, and a scattering or basil leaves.

• Per serving 213 kcalories, protein 8g, carbohydrate 14g, fat 14g, saturated fat 7g, fibre 4g, sugar 13g, salt 1.15g

Blast away the cobwebs with this spicy broth. The best Thai curry pastes come in large pots and can seem costly, but they last ages and taste fantastic, so your taste buds will thank you for it!

Spicy prawn soup

1 tbsp sunflower oil
300g bag crunchy stir-fry vegetables
140g/5oz mushrooms, sliced
2 tbsp Thai green curry paste
400g can reduced-fat coconut milk
200ml/7fl oz vegetable or fish stock
300g/10oz medium straight-to-wok noodles
200g bag cooked prawns

Takes 20 minutes • Serves 4 (easily halved)

1 Heat a wok, add the oil, then stir-fry the veg and mushrooms for 2–3 minutes. Remove with a slotted spoon and set aside.
2 Tip the curry paste into the pan and fry for 1 minute. Pour in the coconut milk and stock. Bring to the boil, drop in the noodles and prawns, then reduce the heat and simmer for 4 minutes until the prawns are cooked through. Stir in the veg and serve.

• Per serving 327 kcalories, protein 16g, carbohydrate 32g, fat 17g, saturated fat 10g, fibre 4g, sugar 4g, salt 0.97g

Just when you think there's nothing in the house for dessert, remember this pudding. It's less rich than bread and butter pud, but simpler to make and utterly delicious.

Easiest-ever bread pudding

568g pot fresh custard
150ml/¼ pint milk
140g/5oz white bread
50g/2oz raisins or dried cherries
butter, for greasing
5–7 tbsp caster sugar

Takes 45 minutes • Serves 4

1 Preheat oven to 140°C/fan 120°C/gas 1. Whisk the custard together with the milk. Trim the crusts from the bread, cut into triangles, then place in a large bowl with the raisins or dried cherries. Pour over the custard mixture, then carefully stir everything together so all the pieces of bread are coated. Lightly grease an ovenproof dish with butter, then spoon in the mixture.

2 Cook for 30–35 minutes until there is just a slight wobble in the centre of the custard. Sprinkle over the sugar to cover the surface, then pop under a hot grill for 1–2 minutes until the sugar starts to melt and caramelize.

• Per serving 363 kcalories, protein 7g, carbohydrate 64g, fat 11g, saturated fat 7g, fibre 1g, sugar 47g, salt 0.57g

Great for lunchboxes, breakfast on the run, or just with a cup of coffee. These will keep for up to a week in an airtight tin.

Cinnamon berry granola bars

100g/4oz butter, plus extra for greasing
200g/8oz porridge oats
100g/4oz sunflower seeds
50g/2oz sesame seeds
50g/2oz chopped walnuts
3 tbsp honey
100g/4oz light muscovado sugar
1 tsp ground cinnamon
100g/4oz dried cranberries, cherries or blueberries (or a mix)

Takes 45 minutes • Makes 12

1 Preheat oven to 160°C/fan 140°C/gas 3. Butter and line the base of a 18cm x 25cm tin. Mix together the oats, seeds and nuts in a roasting tin, then place in the oven for 5–10 minutes to toast.

2 Meanwhile, warm the butter, honey and sugar in a pan, stirring until the butter is melted. Add the oat mix, cinnamon and dried fruit, then mix until all the oats are well coated. Tip into the tin, press down lightly, then bake for 30 minutes. Cool in the tin, then cut into 12 bars.

• Per bar 294 kcalories, protein 6g, carbohydrate 30g, fat 17g, saturated fat 6g, fibre 3g, sugar 17g, salt 0.14g

Don't chuck out overripe bananas – make a delicious banana cake instead. Perfect with a cup of tea, any time of day.

Banana cake with nutty crumble crunch

250g/9oz golden caster sugar
250g/9oz self-raising flour
140g/5oz pecan nuts, walnuts or hazelnuts, roughly chopped
1 tbsp butter, chopped
2 eggs, beaten, plus 2 egg whites
3 large ripe bananas, or 4 small, mashed
150ml/¼ pint sunflower oil
100ml/3½fl oz milk
1 tsp cinnamon
1 tsp baking powder

Takes 1 hour 20 minutes • Serves 10

1 Preheat oven to 180°C/fan 160°C/gas 4, and line the base and sides of a deep 20cm cake tin with non-stick baking paper. Stir together 2 tablespoons each of the sugar, flour and nuts, then add the butter and rub in to make sticky crumbs for the topping.
2 Whisk the egg whites until just stiff. Mix the whole eggs with the bananas, oil and milk. In a large bowl, mix the remaining sugar, flour and nuts with the cinnamon and baking powder. Tip the banana mix into the dry ingredients and quickly stir. Fold in the egg whites, then pour the mixture into the tin. Scatter over the topping and bake for 1 hour until a skewer inserted in the centre comes out clean. After 45 minutes, if the surface is browning too quickly, cover with baking paper.
3 Leave in the tin for 5 minutes, then finish cooling on a wire rack.

• Per serving 476 kcalories, protein 6.6g, carbohydrate 56.2g, fat 26.6g, saturated fat 3.9g, fibre 1.9g, sugar 36g, salt 0.5g

This has all the flavour of a special fruit cake, but won't take ages to make. Grated apple makes it moist, like a carrot cake.

Quick and easy fruit cake

200g/8oz butter, softened, plus extra for greasing
200g/8oz dark muscovado sugar
3 eggs, beaten
1 tbsp black treacle
200g/8oz self-raising flour
2 tsp mixed spice
1 tsp baking powder
2 eating apples, grated (approx. 100g/3½oz each)
300g/10oz mixed sultanas and raisins

Takes about 1 hour • Serves 12

1 Preheat oven to 180°C/fan 160°C/gas 4. Butter and line the bottom of a deep, 20cm round cake tin with greaseproof paper. Beat the first seven ingredients together in a large bowl (electric hand-beaters are best for this), until pale and thick. Using a large metal spoon, gently fold in the dried fruit until evenly combined.

2 Spoon the batter into the tin and bake for 50 minutes–1 hour or until the cake is dark golden, springy to the touch and has shrunk away from the side of the tin slightly.
A skewer inserted into the centre will come out clean when it's ready. Cool completely before decorating. Will keep, wrapped in an airtight container or iced, for up to a week, or can be frozen un-iced for up to a month. Defrost fully before decorating.

• Per slice 350 kcalories, protein 4g, carbohydrate 51g, fat 16g, saturated fat 9g, fibre 1g, added sugar 18g, salt 0.63g

An old-fashioned homely bake, perfect with tea or for dessert.

Spiced apple cake

140g/5oz softened butter
200g/8oz caster sugar
2 eggs, beaten
200g/8oz self-raising flour
½ tsp ground cloves
¼ tsp grated nutmeg
450g/1lb Bramley apples, peeled,
cored and thickly sliced
icing sugar, for dusting

Takes 2 hours • Serves 12

1 Preheat oven to 180°C/fan 160°C/gas 4, then butter and line a deep, 20cm round cake tin. Put the butter and sugar into a large bowl and beat together until pale and creamy. Beat in the eggs, a little at a time, until light and fluffy. Mix the flour with the cloves and nutmeg, then fold into the eggy mixture.
2 Spread half the mix over the bottom of the tin, then cover with the apple slices. Dot the rest of the mix over the apples, then bake for 1½ hours or until a skewer inserted into the centre comes out clean. It will get quite dark on the top before it's done in the middle. Leave the cake in the tin to cool (it might sink a bit), then dust with icing sugar to serve.

• Per serving 238 kcalories, protein 3g, carbohydrate 34g, fat 11g, saturated fat 6g, fibre 1g, sugar 22g, salt 0.37g

It's easy to make a good loaf of bread – and cut your shopping bills into the bargain. This recipe can be easily doubled or tripled, and the spare loaves can be frozen.

Classic white loaf

500g/1lb 2oz strong white flour, plus extra for rolling and dusting
7g sachet fast-action yeast
1 tsp salt
up to 350ml/12fl oz lukewarm water
a little sunflower oil, for greasing

Takes about 1 hour, plus rising
Cuts into 16 slices

1 Tip the flour, yeast and salt into a large bowl and make a well in the middle. Pour in most of the water and mix to a slightly wet dough. Tip out on to a lightly floured surface and knead for 10 minutes or until smooth and elastic. Place in a clean, oiled bowl, cover and leave until doubled in size.

2 Preheat oven to 220°C/fan 200°C/gas 7. Knock back the dough by tipping it out on to a floured surface and kneading it a little. Shape the dough into a rugby ball and place in an oiled 900g loaf tin. Cover loosely and leave to prove until risen and pillowy. Dust with flour and slash the top, if you like. Bake for 15 minutes, then lower the oven temperature to 190°C/fan 170°C/gas 5 and bake for 30 minutes more until the dough is dark golden and sounds hollow when removed from the tin and tapped on the base. Cool completely on a rack.

• Per slice 111 kcalories, protein 4g, carbohydrate 24g, fat 1g, saturated fat none, fibre 1g, sugar 1g, salt 0.31g

Add seeds, nuts and wholemeal flour to a basic dough for a bread with bags of flavour and that's full of goodness. The loaf will stay fresh in an airtight container for 3 days or can be frozen for 1 month.

Malted nut and seed loaf

100g/4oz mixed seeds (we used a mix of linseeds, hemp seeds, pumpkin seeds and sesame seeds)
500g/1lb 2oz strong wholemeal flour
7g sachet fast-action yeast
1 tsp salt
50g/2oz walnut pieces
up to 350ml/12fl oz lukewarm water
a little sunflower oil, for greasing

Takes 1 hour, plus rising • Cuts into 12 slices

1 Set aside 1 tablespoon of seeds, then mix all the dry ingredients together in a large bowl and make a well in the middle. Stir in the seeds and nuts. Pour in the water and mix to a slightly wet dough. Tip out on to a lightly floured surface and knead for 10 minutes or until smooth and elastic. Put in a clean, oiled bowl, cover and leave until doubled in size. Roll the dough around in the remaining seeds, then lift the bread on to a tray to prove for about 30 minutes until doubled in size.
2 Preheat oven to 220°C/fan 200°C/gas 7. Bake the bread for 15 minutes, then lower the oven temperature to 190°C/fan 170°C/gas 5 and continue to bake for 30 minutes until the loaf sounds hollow when removed from the tin and tapped on the base. Leave on a wire rack to cool completely.

• Per slice 172 kcalories, protein 7g, carbohydrate 28g, fat 4g, saturated fat 1g, fibre 5g, sugar 1g, salt 0.43g

You'll love these savoury buns for breakfast, brunch, or your lunchbox. The secret to light muffins is to stop mixing before you think you should.

Cheddar and bacon buns

1 tsp oil, plus extra for greasing
4 rashers streaky bacon, cut into small pieces
50g/2oz mature cheddar
175g/6oz plain flour
1 tsp baking powder
1 tsp English mustard
2 eggs
85g/3oz butter, melted
200ml/7fl oz milk
1 tbsp parsley, chopped

Takes 40 minutes • Makes 6 large buns

1 Preheat oven to 180°C/fan 160°C/gas 4, and grease 6 wells of a muffin tin with a little oil.
2 Heat the oil in a frying pan and fry the bacon until crisp. Tip out on to kitchen paper and allow to cool. Cut two-thirds of the cheese into little pieces and finely grate the rest.
3 Sift the flour, baking powder, ½ teaspoon of salt and a little pepper into a bowl. Whisk the mustard, eggs, butter, and milk in a jug. Pour the wet mix into the dry and stir a few times until just combined. Add the bacon, cheese pieces and parsley, being careful not to overwork the mix.
4 Spoon into the greased wells (they will be quite full), sprinkle each with a little grated cheese, then bake for 25 minutes or until golden, risen and firm to the touch.

• Per bun 322 kcalories, protein 12g, carbohydrate 25g, fat 20g, saturated fat 11g, fibre 1g, sugar 2g, salt 1.63g

It can be hard to find special gluten-free ingredients, so this cake uses a cheap and starchy staple that almost everyone has knocking about in the kitchen.

Gluten-free lemon drizzle cake

200g/8oz butter, softened, plus extra for greasing
200g/8oz golden caster sugar
4 eggs
175g/6oz ground almonds
250g/9oz mashed potatoes, cold
zest of 3 lemons
2 tsp gluten-free baking powder

FOR THE DRIZZLE
4 tbsp granulated sugar
juice of 1 lemon

Takes 1 hour 10 minutes • Serves 8–10

1 Preheat oven to 180°C/fan 160°C/gas 4. Butter and line a deep, 20cm round cake tin. Beat the sugar and butter together until light and fluffy, then gradually add the eggs, beating after each addition. Fold in the almonds, cold mashed potato, lemon zest and baking powder.

2 Tip the mixture into the tin, level the top, then bake for 40–45 minutes or until golden and a skewer inserted into the centre of the cake comes out clean. Turn out on to a wire rack after 10 minutes' cooling.

3 Mix the granulated sugar and the lemon juice together, then spoon over the top of the cake, letting it drip down the sides. Allow the cake to cool completely before slicing.

• Per serving (10) 514 kcalories, protein 9g, carbohydrate 41g, fat 36g, saturated fat 2g, fibre 2g, sugar 35g, salt 0.88g

This rustic bake is based on a cake from Tuscany and is a great new way to use grapes. Try eating it warm with a scoop of ice cream for pudding.

Citrus grape cake

175ml/6fl oz olive oil, plus extra for greasing
200g/8oz plain flour, plus 1 tbsp for dusting
200g/8oz light muscovado sugar
100g/4oz softened butter
3 eggs
zest of 1 orange
zest of 1 lemon
75ml/2½fl oz of milk
1 tsp baking powder
175g/6oz grapes, halved and seeded
4–5 tbsp demerara sugar

Takes 1 hour • Serves 8–10

1 Preheat oven to 180°C/fan 160°C/gas 4. Oil a 23cm springform cake tin, tip in 1 tablespoon of flour and shake all over the pan until covered. Discard any excess flour. Beat the sugar and butter until creamy and well combined. Add the eggs, one at a time, then stir through the orange and lemon zests. Stir together the milk and olive oil, then pour into the mix. Tip in the flour and baking powder, and beat everything together briefly until smooth.

2 Spoon the cake batter into the prepared tin, then smooth the surface with the back of the spoon. Scatter the halved grapes over the top, then sprinkle over the extra sugar. Bake for 45–50 minutes until a skewer inserted into the centre of the cake comes out clean. Eat warm or cool.

• Per serving 574 kcalories, protein 6g, carbohydrate 62g, fat 33g, saturated fat 10g, fibre 1g, sugar 39g, salt 0.49g

Good old cocoa powder makes this family cake as chocolatey as is needs to be – and works out a lot cheaper than using 70per cent plain chocolate.

Chocolate marble cake

225g/8oz butter, softened
225g/8oz caster sugar
4 eggs
225g/8oz self-raising flour
3 tbsp milk
1 tsp vanilla extract
2 tbsp cocoa powder, sifted

Takes 1 hour 10 minutes • Serves 8

1 Preheat oven to 180°C/fan 160°C/gas 4. Grease and line a round 20cm cake tin. Beat the butter and sugar together. Add the eggs, one at a time, mixing well after each addition. Fold through the flour, milk, and vanilla extract until the mixture is smooth.

2 Divide the mixture between 2 bowls. Stir the cocoa powder into the mixture in one of the bowls. Dollop the chocolate and vanilla cake mixes into the cake tin alternately. When all the mixture has been used up, tap the bottom of the tin on the work surface to remove any air bubbles. Take a skewer and swirl it around the mixture in the tin a few times to create a marbled effect.

3 Bake the cake for 45–55 minutes until a skewer inserted into the centre comes out clean. Turn out on to a cooling rack and leave to cool.

• Per serving 468 kcalories, protein 6g, carbohydrate 52g, fat 27g, saturated fat 16g, fibre 1g, sugar 31g, salt 0.81g

This special cake will go perfectly with coffee or makes a dessert to die for when served warm with ice cream. If maple syrup seems a little extravagant, use a little squeezy toffee sauce instead.

Toffee pecan cake

300g/10oz pecan nut halves
140g/5oz stoned dates
200g/8oz butter, softened, plus extra for greasing
200g/8oz light muscovado sugar
1 tsp mixed spice
4 eggs, beaten
140g/5oz self-raising flour
maple syrup, to serve

Takes 55 minutes • Serves 8

1 Tip 100g/3½oz of the pecans into a food processor and whiz until fine. Tip out into a bowl and set aside.

2 Put the dates into a small pan with enough water to cover, boil for 5 minutes until very soft, then drain, discarding the liquid, and whiz in the food processor until smooth.

3 Preheat oven to 160°C/ fan 140°C/gas 4. Butter and line the base of a round 20cm cake tin. Beat together the butter, sugar and spice until light and creamy, then tip in the dates, ground pecans, eggs and a pinch of salt, and beat briefly until smooth.

4 Fold in the flour with a metal spoon, then spoon into the tin and level the top. Sprinkle the remaining nuts over the top (don't press them in) then bake for 40 minutes or until risen and golden and a skewer inserted into the centre comes out clean. Serve warm, with generous drizzles of maple syrup.

• Per serving 692 kcalories, protein 10g, carbohydrate 53g, fat 51g, saturated fat 16g, fibre 3g, sugar 39g, salt 0.68g

Kids absolutely adore these!

Smarties cookies

350g/12oz plain flour
1 tsp bicarbonate of soda
1 tsp baking powder
250g/9oz butter, softened
300g/10oz caster sugar
1 egg, beaten
1 tsp vanilla extract
2 × 40g tubes Smarties

Takes 30 minutes • Makes 10 large cookies

1 Preheat oven to 180°C/fan 160°C/gas 4. Sift the flour, bicarbonate of soda, baking powder and a pinch of salt into a mixing bowl, then set aside. Cream together the butter and sugar until pale and fluffy, then beat in the egg and vanilla extract. Gradually beat in the sifted dry ingredients to form a stiff dough.

2 Roll the dough into 10 balls, then place on baking sheets, spaced well apart. Press several Smarties into each ball, flattening them slightly. Bake for 15 minutes until pale golden brown. Leave for 2 minutes to firm up a little, then transfer to wire racks to cool completely. Will keep in an airtight tin for up to 3 days.

• Per cookie 253 kcalories, protein 3g, carbohydrate 35g, fat 12g, saturated fat 7g, fibre 1g, sugar 22g, salt 0.47g

This foolproof recipe will give you a sponge cake that's light as a feather. If it's a special occasion, it's worth splashing out on fresh cream – the end result will be better than any cake you can buy.

Classic sponge sandwich

200g/8oz soft butter, plus extra
for greasing
200g/8oz self-raising flour
1 tsp baking powder
200g/8oz golden caster sugar
4 eggs
2 tbsp milk
icing sugar, for dusting

FOR THE FILLING
142ml pot double cream
50g/2oz golden caster sugar
½ tsp vanilla extract
100g/4oz strawberry jam

Takes 40 minutes • Cuts into 8

1 Preheat oven to 180°C/fan 160°C/gas 4. Grease and base-line two 20cm round, non-stick, sandwich tins with baking paper, then lightly grease again.
2 Sift the flour and baking powder into a large bowl, then tip in all the other sponge ingredients. Using an electric whisk, beat everything together until smooth. Divide the mix between the cake tins, then bake for 20–25 minutes until springy and golden. When cool enough to handle, remove the cakes from the tins, then leave to cool completely on a rack.
3 To make the filling, whip the cream with the caster sugar and vanilla extract until it holds its shape. Build the cake by spreading the top of one sponge with jam and the bottom of the other with cream. Sandwich the two together, then dust the top with icing sugar.

• Per slice 568 kcalories, protein 7g, carbohydrate 62g, fat 34g, saturated fat 20g, fibre 1g, sugar 43g, salt 0.94g

Index